The Good Moms, Their Children and Friendship

The Good Moms, Their Children and Friendship

Patricia Dutt

1. Biography. 2. Immigrants – Immigration.

3. Iran 4. Spirituality 5 Grief – Death. 6. Women's Studies.

7. New York State.

Copyright ©2021 by Patricia Dutt

All rights reserved.
ISBN-9798756230888

No part of this book may be used or reproduced in any manner without the written permission of the author except for brief quotations.

Jacket Design by Diana Ozolins

For Anna, Laura, Ben and Z.

Table of Contents

Introduction   9

Part 1: Nasrin

1. Family and Friends in Chronological Order   15
   - Map of Iran   16
2. Early life in Iran, 1959-1981   17
3. Early Years in the US, 1981-1986   19
4. Life as a Single Mom, West Hill, 1986-1991   24
5. Becoming a Citizen   28
6. Life on West Hill, 1991-1994   30
7. Life on West Hill, Hook Place, 1994-2003   33
8. Nasrin's Iran, 1992-2018   36
9. Life on East Hill, 2003-2015   41
10. Living with Cancer, 2016-2019   43

Part 2: Immigrants, Immigrants and Iran

1. Immigrants   53
2. Immigration   55
3. Iranians in the US   59
4. Amol, Mazandaran Province, Iran   61
5. Iran: The Past   64
6. Iran: The Present   68
7. The 1979 Hostage Crisis   71

Part 3: Reflections After Death

1. Spirituality, Mourning and Grief   81
2. Death   91
3. Friendship   97

   Afterward July 22, 2021   112
   References   114
   Appendix: The Interviews   119
   Acknowledgments   228

Introduction:

The Good Moms, Their Children and Friendship

My close friend, Nasrin, an immigrant and single mom, passed away in the spring of 2019. Her presence in the world had not only changed my life, but the lives of many others. This became clear to me during Nasrin's memorial service as I listened to a myriad of testimonials of friendship and love. I felt a strong need to honor Nasrin, an unassuming woman who carved out a life for herself and her daughter, Zahara, and so I decided to write about her. What she achieved seemed monumental to me, especially given the American hostility toward Iranians starting in the late seventies, a hostility that continues in some parts of the US to this day. She defied the odds and every last one of us who called ourselves her friend admired her tenacity and warmth.

I knew Nasrin only from what I experienced during our friendship. Another friend, a writer like myself, asserted that *People want to tell their stories*, and so armed with these ideas, I forged ahead and began contacting Nasrin's friends and family, asking if they would consent to an interview that would be recorded and perhaps turned into a book. *No one ever felt worse after writing*, the poet Naomi Shahib Nye has said.

I personally interviewed 22 people. Because some participants expressed a desire to return to Iran, I omitted surnames and changed the names of some institutions and cities. Each interview represented a relationship formed by two individuals, each its own contained record, so I kept the interviews whole (editing them for clarity and redundancy) and have included them at the end of the book, as the sole appendix. Every single person I interviewed, without exception, had something surprising and vital to say about Nasrin, and about life. For some, the interviews appeared to be cathartic; for me, as I listened to them, I often thought: yes, this is how I felt and what I thought, and how wonderfully this individual has articulated this emotion.

Initially I collected the interviews with the intent of sharing them with Zahara and Nasrin's friends, but after some reflection, it seemed possible to write a small biography of Nasrin (Part I). Then as I re-read the interviews, they began to raise questions that required context. For instance, after the first interview with Hashem, Nasrin's brother, I realized I knew nothing about the city of Amol, where Nasrin's family still resides. I searched for information and wrote a few pages about Amol. Then what did I know about the country of Iran? Not much. What did I really know about the 1979 Hostage Crisis? This information makes-up Part II.

Then the term spirituality came up, as would be expected with the subject of death. What were some of its contours? Honestly, I had not thought much about the term before Nasrin's death. What about grief? Death itself? The idea was not to write a literary or scholarly treatise, but to do some research, pay attention to what I read and listened to on podcasts, take notes, then reflect and give more depth to the questions raised. This formed Part III along with a section on friendship. Thus, Nasrin's chronological life, based on facts gleaned from the interviews, formed the book's backbone, and this backbone I fleshed out with content on immigration, Iran, spirituality and so on. I hoped that those readers who only knew Iran from the American news media would gain a fuller appreciation of the country and its people.

Writing this book gave me the opportunity to set aside time and space to contemplate a life completed on this earth, and by extension, contemplate my own life, and what I envisioned and hoped for in my remaining years. By understanding and appreciating another human being I suspected that I'd shed light on the *who-am-I*, the question that most of us ask all of our lives in one way or another. It follows that in making an assessment of Nasrin's life, I have made an assessment of my own life.

I needed to write this now and not wait until I retired, or *until the time was right*. The time is never right. And it's a practical matter that memories fade and that we move on to other projects. My focus and urge was to contemplate the ideas of love, spirituality, death and friendship. So you write about an idea, set it aside for a few weeks or months, look at it later, let it sit again so it gains resonance, and maybe another idea falls into place and before you know it these ideas connect. You dig a little deeper into your subject.

While this book is about Nasrin, her close friends, our children and our interwoven relationships, it is also about gifts that ensue from fully living life. When I started interviewing people, I was not sure what else the book would entail, where it would go, or how it would end. It sounds like the trajectory of a life.

I met Nasrin in the fall of 1997, having moved to New York state a year earlier. Nasrin, who was picking up her young daughter, Zahara, on her way home from her job, was standing in my hallway with that soft, late-afternoon sun on her mahogany hair, and she seemed to me to be not only movie-star gorgeous, but gracious and wise. I felt to be the opposite. The house in which the two of us stood was not the house I wanted to live in. Only after signing and depositing five thousand dollars (a lot of money back then) did I understand that our real estate taxes were no small amount, and would rise exponentially. I should have known better. I would have forfeited the down-payment but my husband made most crucial decisions back then, and when the real estate agent threatened us with a lawsuit if we broke the contract, he – and we – withdrew our request. We had been living in the Midwest for 10 years and I was accustomed to friendlier, less-calculating people. We selected the Depression-era house because our three children could walk to all of the schools. The house was solidly built and came with a barn (which had been remolded into a garage), and it had the most wonderful office for me. The office was filled with cherrywood bookshelves. It had a French gliding glass door that locked, and it was set off from the rest of the house and surrounded by tall trees.

As Nasrin and I stood there waiting for the girls, she marveled at the house's craftmanship, and its kitchen with two walls of windows, but what I saw was instability, and a growing desire to leave a marital situation that had become increasingly inflexible. It would not be easy:

I had made only one close friend and my family lived a thousand miles away.

"Do you have any other kids?" I said to Nasrin. Zahara and Anna (my daughter), were three months apart in age and had recently met in the fourth grade. This was the third school Anna had been to in a little more than 18 months, and she was miserable. Sensing her despondency and outsider status, Zahara invited her into her friend group.

"Just me and Zahara," Nasrin said casually.

I understood immediately what she meant. And from her accent I correctly surmised that she hadn't been born here, so whatever she was doing, well it must not be easy. Of course I wondered: how was she managing without a spouse or a partner? There she stood a few feet from me: calm, friendly and graceful. My first impression of Nasrin. I did not know she was Iranian – not that it would have made any difference to our friendship – but I had never met an Iranian. I had not owned a TV since 1980 and I certainly did not consider myself worldly.

A month later, when I went to get my yearly mammogram, the boob-squeezing technician, to my surprise was none other than Nasrin: smiling warmly, as if we'd known each other for years.

Part I: Nasrin

Family and Friends in Chronological Order

Following is a list of Nasrin's family (her brother) and friends (many) and the date and/or circumstances under which they met. For detailed information, see the appendix for each respondent's interview.

- Hashem: Nasrin's brother, Amol, Iran.
- Sue: 1986, Nasrin replied to an apartment newspaper ad listing an apartment for rent in Iliad; lived with Sue for several years.
- Zahara: Nasrin's daughter, born in 1987, in Iliad.
- Carolyn: 1988/89, met while Nasrin was walking Zahara in a stroller.
- Debbie: 1988-89, Nasrin replied to newspaper ad, worked for Debbie for two years.
- Noni: 1989, met through a neighbor; daughters are friends too.
- Alice: (mother) and Hannah (daughter), 1989, met through Noni.
- Virginia: 1991, met Nasrin at the elementary school, also lived on West Hill, Iliad.
- Susan: 1992, met Nasrin at a party of Carolyn's.
- Anna: 1997, met Zahara in fourth grade.
- Pat: 1997, Anna's Mom, met through Anna, and Guthrie.
- Ben: 1997, Anna's brother, met through Pat and Anna.
- Zhila: 1998, met at Guthrie and through their children.
- Yasamin: about 1998, met at the university's Middle Eastern group.
- Carole and April (mother and daughter): 2001, met through Virginia's daughter.
- Sorayya: about 2008, met on East Hill, also at a party of Pat's.
- Adam: 2013, met Zahara at graduate school, in San Diego.
- Marie: 2013, met on a walking trail.
- Julia and Shiv: 2018, met Nasrin at their wedding, London, however, Julia's Mom and Nasrin were close cousins.

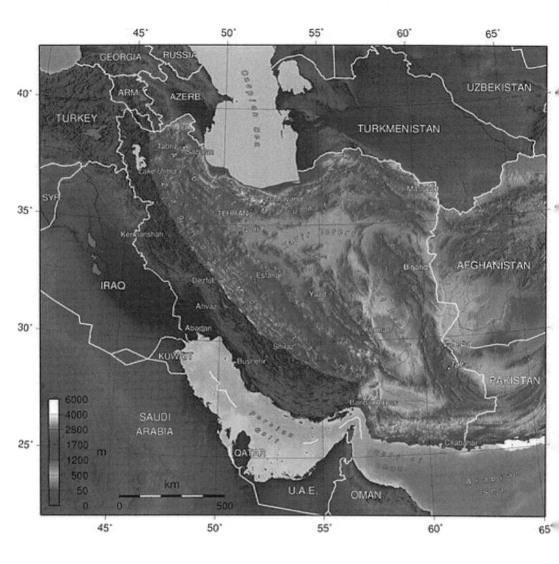

Iran in the world. Amol is north of Tehran, near the Caspian Sea.
(https://commons.wikimedia.org/wiki
/File:Persian_plateau_topo_en.jpg)[1]

Early Life in Iran, 1959-1981

I do not have much information on Nasrin's life in Iran, and for the most part, relied on a single interview with her brother, Hashem, and Zahara's memories; even so, the language barrier with Hashem (the interview was translated in real time at a grocery store by Hashem's son) certainly impacted the interview's flow. The interview was short because of tight schedules and Hashem's quick departure back to Iran. Hashem's son declined an interview; Iranians, especially those still living in both Iran and the US, were hesitant to share much information, given the possibility of jeopardizing future travel.

Nasrin was born in 1959, in Amol, a city between the Elburz Mountains and the Caspian Sea, and lived there until her early twenties. Her father, a successful businessman, owned real estate, farms and ships. Her mother followed a traditional path and raised four children: two girls and two boys.

"My mom," Zahara said, "was very close to her family and cousins and they all lived in one house together. There were lots of kids. There was a house in Amol and another along the Caspian Sea." Nasrin's father died of colon cancer when he was 60. Nasrin was 14, and after that, money was not so plentiful, and Nasrin, being the eldest, assumed a major role in family care-giving. Even as a child, according to Hashem, Nasrin "Was a humble kid. She worried about the rest of the family and their success. She didn't bother anyone, but she did give advice, even as a kid. And she didn't like liars. Everyone had so much respect for her."

At the same time, although the family/extended family were in business, Nasrin, being an energetic and devoted learner, wanted to attend college. In fact, she was the only sibling who did, and she graduated from a three-year college with a degree in biology. Hashem said: "She loved school and studying. She was made for it."

For a few years after college she taught health classes in the schools. Then in the early 80's she emigrated from Iran to marry a man whom the family knew, Bahman. Before Bahman, she'd had a serious boyfriend. No one knows exactly why the relationship fell apart, but Nasrin did travel with this man later in life, after he divorced his wife.

Early Years in the US, 1982-1986

Henceforth, *many* friends from Iliad contributed to the biographical information that I collected on Nasrin's life, and as would be expected, there was not always agreement on how her life unfolded. Some possible explanations include that memories fade, interpretations of the same event can vary, and sometimes people even hear the spoken word differently. No one seems to understand the latter better than Daniel Kahneman, psychologist and Nobel prize winner in Economic Sciences, 2002. He describes how the mind's bias can rewire incoming thoughts. To illustrate this point, he offers an anecdote: he and his wife were at a party and she stated that a friend of theirs was "sexy" because "He undressed the maid himself."[2] Kahneman responded with a surprised: "What?" and she repeated: "He underestimates himself." For a more detailed examination of the mind's inner workings, see Kahneman's Ted Talk on *The Riddle of Experience Versus Memory* or his book, *Thinking, Fast and Slow*.

Thus, I did not alter the accounts of Nasrin that I recorded and transcribed, at least not consciously.

Nasrin emigrated to the US a year after she married Bahman, a family acquaintance. She married him over the phone from Iran in 1981 or 1982, and would have married him three years sooner were it not for the Iranian Revolution. Nasrin initially lived in with Bahman in Los Angeles – a fact I became aware of only after her passing – for five years. Then the couple moved to Iliad. Bahman, a PhD candidate, apparently a brilliant man, had been living in Los Angeles in an Iranian community where he studied physics. According to Nasrin's first Iliad friend, Sue: "Bahman was 10 years older than Nasrin. He spotted her and said: *I want to marry her.*" Nasrin was not just beautiful, like many Iranian wo men, she was movie-star beautiful. She had incredible, large dark eyes and was not shy about holding another's gaze.

"Her marriage was arranged," Debbie, who hired Nasrin to watch her sons, said. "He was from the family."

While living in Los Angeles, Nasrin had some Iranian friends and worked in a department store, but not much is known about this period of her life. I could not find anyone who knew her in Los Angeles. She did not speak much English. Did she have American friends? Americans were still angry over the 1979 Hostage Crisis and for the most part, had little unbiased media information on the incident's back story. Many Americans were anti-Iranian. Zahara mentioned that it was probably a very lonely time for her mother, especially given that Bahman was "somewhat controlling." Nasrin never spoke much about those five years of her life with any of her friends.

Still, she viewed the US as a country with opportunity, and a country that offered new beginnings to those who were fearless and worked hard.

"Nasrin could not go into the family business [in Iran]," Debbie said. "It was not acceptable. Life was very traditional and Nasrin didn't like that. These were weird times in Iran: sometimes a woman could be educated, sometimes not. It depended on the regime. Same thing with the young, and going out in public and being covered up and the bullshit about the arranged marriage. She was a woman, and you could only do so much. She didn't have a choice. She had to follow her husband, but Nasrin was an independent woman."

How much did she know about the US? "I don't think she knew much about it," Zahara said. "It was this idealized place in her mind but she was really excited to move here. But there were a lot of things that were very different for her because she had only lived in Iran. Iran was a sterner society after the Revolution. So it was all a shock. It was very different."

"You know the popular image of the US would be that it was this wonderful place, this Land of Plenty," Carolyn said. [Nasrin and Carolyn met when Zahara was an infant.] "She didn't come from a poor family--they were well-to do. You were going to go and your situation is going to get better." Carolyn was also born in Iran. "It actually happened to my family too: there was this magical image as to what this place was like. There couldn't be anything wrong here."

"I think every Middle Easterner knows about the US in some shape or form," Yasamin, another immigrant, said. "You never really know what a place is like until you move and live there. She knew some, but the depth of details and what life would be like for her, no. But none of us do."

Bahman then obtained a post-doc at a university in the east, and they moved to New York State in February 1986. They initially lived in a hotel in Iliad, then answered a newspaper ad for a basement apartment. That was the beginning of Nasrin's friendship with the people of Iliad. According to Sue, who with her husband rented their apartment to Nasrin and Bahman: "I was hesitant about a couple living here who did not speak much English, but it turned out to be the best thing that happened because she helped me so much. I've had MS symptoms since '76, diagnosed in '79. So we got very close. Nasrin was up here all the time, she used to bathe Laura, my one-year-old, and my son, who was four. She was just there."

About 10 months later, Bahman apparently secured a position in Canada, so they did not renew their lease and Sue rented the apartment to another tenant. Bahman's job, however, fell through, so Sue and her husband rented an upstairs room to the couple. Nasrin would spend a good portion of her day cooking, not only for herself and Bahman, but for Sue's family too. Sue's kids wanted to be with Nasrin, in fact Nasrin often watched *Sesame Street* with them. At this time Bahman was working on his PhD, but not working at a job, and although their families gave them some support, they did not have a lot of money. "We thought it would be just a couple of weeks," Sue said. "Then after they moved upstairs, Nasrin was not feeling well – turns out she was pregnant with Zahara. Her husband was not around, turned out he was at CU where he previously worked playing pool, and things like that." There were some heated discussions between Sue and Bahman about the next step.

Eventually Nasrin and Bahman moved to another basement apartment, this one on Comfort Road. Nasrin was "pretty much on her own." Her husband was "not whatsoever supportive of her," Sue said. After Zahara was born, they continued to live on Comfort Road. "So she was stuck at this place and couldn't go anywhere. There wasn't any bus, and she didn't drive, and living in that part of town wasn't good for her. The apartment had high basement windows and one time she found a snake down there. Things like that." Still, to contribute to the finances, Nasrin walked "miles to catch a bus with a newborn (Zahara)" for a job, which was watching twins who were a year or two older than Zahara.

Nasrin would also secure Zahara in a stroller, taking her on walks, and on one walk, she met Carolyn. Carolyn heard from a neighbor that another Iranian woman was living on Comfort road. "I thought I don't know if I want to meet another Iranian. I think Nasrin felt the same; we thought it might be kind of show-offy, and neither of us were in that mode. But then I met Nasrin walking, strolling Zahara down the roadside, who at the time was one-and-a-half-years-old, and we had to talk. We knew who each other was, so we introduced ourselves. We became fast friends. For more than 30 years, till she passed away. I just adored her. She didn't have a bad bone in her body."

Around this time, Nasrin happened to stroll Zahara past a building where Bahman's car was parked. When questioned about this incident, Bahman admitted to having an affair with a graduate student. According to Sue: "Bahman told her, 'I found this girl or woman (a student he used to tutor) who said she'll marry me so I can get a green card.'" Bahman and Nasrin divorced, and Bahman married his student and they moved to California.

He left Nasrin nearly penniless.

Life as a Single Mom on West Hill, 1987-1991

After Bahman left, Sue introduced Nasrin to Nancy (there is no interview with Nancy, she passed away), who rented Nasrin another basement apartment, this one on West Hill, on Richard Place. "She met Nasrin and really liked her, so the two of them (Nasrin and Zahara) moved in," Sue said. "Nasrin ended up, and she was not happy about this, cooking every meal and doing dishes. She also paid some rent and she was babysitting."

"Nasrin lived in the basement of Nancy's apartment," Debbie said. "It was a little dinky, moldy apartment with mildew. It was moist, but she could be independent. Zahara had a thick green mucous coming from her nose and never breathed out of her nose for the first two or three years! It was terrible! Just terrible! She was quite congested. We laugh about it now. But Nancy was a little odd."

Nasrin had to find more substantial work. According to Susan (who met Nasrin at a party of Carolyn's): "She didn't know how to make a bed, much less speak English. They had staff and staff did all the cooking and cleaning until her Dad died when she was 14. She didn't know anything about what she was coming to."

"There was a time when she was working for 75 cents-an-hour," Carolyn said, "and she didn't take any public assistance. Such a smart, determined and ethical person. Honest."

Nasrin began cleaning houses and buildings, and babysitting, and if she could not leave Zahara with Nancy, she took her with her. Many of Nasrin's friends made this point, and I remember Nasrin telling me that when she worked at the hospital, Zahara was often right by her side. "She would talk to me," Zahara said. "And she probably brought along some toys."

Nasrin met her next door neighbor, Kumi, whose daughter, Noni, became a very close friend. "It was probably Nancy who said, 'Oh, you should meet my housemate because she has a daughter similar in age to yours.'" The first time Noni and Nasrin met, Zahara was in a highchair. Maia [Noni's daughter] and Zahara were a year apart, and attended the same public schools."

"My Mom was also an immigrant, and my husband," Noni said. "So I have a lot of experience with people coming to this country and having to readjust to their life, and I think there was a kinship there. There were a lot of things we didn't share opinions on. We would still get together on holidays and birthdays. I have lots of videos of Zahara's birthdays and things like that. Nasrin didn't have a family here and we became her family. In general, my family tends to adopt people, so Nasrin just became part of the family. It was not even a question. I treated her more like a sister than a friend. Even while knitting, I'm swearing at her: *What the hell were you thinking? This is enormous!*" (Comment about a blanket that Noni was finishing for Zahara's son.)

At Kumi's house, she met another friend, Alice. "Hannah was Zahara's age, and they became friends, along with Maia, who was a year younger. And I just remember the three of them, little children playing and just how sweet that was. Nasrin was never anything but sweet."

"I don't think her family had any idea of how she was living," Carolyn said. "I think they assumed anyone here was wealthy. She'd always take a lot of gifts whenever she'd go there [to Iran]. I guess they just assumed she was doing really well. I don't know how she got those jobs but she took Zahara with her until Zahara got into school."

Nasrin continued to babysit, making sometimes only 75 cents an hour: she was an immigrant, possessed no green card and was the sole caregiver of a small child. Then in 1989 (September), back when people read newspapers, Nasrin answered an ad for watching children.

"The first time she came to interview at my house, it was without Zahara," Debbie said. "And she said, 'I have something very serious to share with you, and you might not want to hire me.' And I thought: is she a criminal? 'There are two things: I have been through a divorce, and I have a daughter and I have to bring her with me.' Just like that. And I was okay with that. She started working that next week. That was a big thing: she needed money. I had six weeks maternity leave and she stayed with us until we left Iliad in '91.

"I wasn't sure if they were okay with animals. We had two dogs and two cats, but Nasrin loved dogs, and she was fine with cats, but the cats probably aggravated Zahara's allergies. And she was scared of them, but once she wasn't, she liked the cats. Zahara was really timid as a kid, and she was scared of men. She did not feel comfortable around men (although her playmates were Debbie's sons, Jay and Adam). When we were getting ready to leave for Michigan, Zahara spoke her first word to Bill in those three years, and it was something simple, but he was flabbergasted. It was monumental to him. For some reason we were walking down State Street, meeting at Planned Parenthood, and they were crossing the street and he said: 'Take my hand, look both ways, okay?' And she said, 'Yes, I am fine.' And he was like: 'Oh my God – she spoke to me!' Actually, she probably didn't catch herself in time. It took her a long time to warm up to anything."

"God bless Nasrin for taking care of those three little kids: a newborn, a one-year-old and a two-year-old," Debbie said. "Cute to see them all together, and she did it with grace, and ease and had fun with it. She had an old clunker car, and was nervous about taking the three kids. So when she was able to afford a better car, she asked to take the kids out, and I said, 'Okay!' All those kids in car seats. They would go on outings and field trips. We also had strollers and the kids walked."

Sue: "I taught Nasrin how to drive. I think she had driven some at home, but it might have been a stick shift. We didn't have to work at it too long. I don't know anything about the first car, I don't even know what it was! She would find cars that didn't cost a lot. I remember she got one that was sitting here in Pete's parking lot, and she went in and asked about that. I don't even know if it had a *For Sale* sign on it. She did end up buying that car. They might not have lasted her long, but she found cars."

"I remember that my husband was helping her with the car," Virginia said. Virginia and Nasrin met on West Hill – their daughters being the same age. "Her car wouldn't start in the morning. It was a very old car. Winter in Iliad, imagine! Not fun. She had friends who helped her, but she struggled."

"Why don't you fight him for child support?" Sue asked Nasrin. "'Oh no', Nasrin said, 'because he'll want to split custody and I don't want that to happen.'"

Nasrin continued to babysit for Debbie. "There's a story about Nasrin putting one of the plastic kiddie pools in the front yard. It was flat there. There was this pudgy, pale red-haired boy, Luke. A lot of baby fat. They all wanted to swim, so she put the four kids in the pool. Luke didn't have a suit but he wanted to swim and Nas didn't want his clothes to get wet, so he just went in. He had one of these disappearing penises. Nasrin and I laughed our butts off over that. She had a great sense of humor. All I needed her to do was watch the kids, she also had the laundry done, the dinner cooked. She'd take the kids up to Flaccos farm and watch the horses and pick up treasures around the fence. All sorts of things. I'd come home exhausted and she'd have dinner on the stove, and I'd say, 'Oh honey!!' And she'd say: 'Not a problem.' We'd never had Iranian food before. She was a godsend."

Becoming a US Citizen

According to Debbie: "Nasrin had an arranged marriage with butthead. She was on a visa related to his visa, and if she was divorced, she could have been deported, and she did not want to be deported. She did not want to take Zahara to live there. She applied for citizenship. Early in the divorce she had to prove that butthead still lived with her; immigration came in and looked for clothes in the closets and toothbrushes, but this was at the transition of the divorce, and I think he refused to move out. It was not a good time."

"The police came to the door and arrested Nasrin because she was here illegally. They found out about the divorce," Sue said. "I don't know if Nancy lent her money to get out of jail. How did the police find out? I think because they got divorced and they knew she was here. He probably had a visa – that's how he was over here for school."

"INS or the police, came to her house in the middle of the night," Sorayya, who met Nasrin on East Hill, said. "Zahara was really small and she begged them to allow her to show up at the police station in the morning or wherever she had to go. Somehow that was arranged and she was told by a lawyer or friend that it would be almost impossible to get residency given her situation. There was this one chance: if she could show a judge (I don't know if this was a stipulation for Iranians) that she was doing everything to better herself and provide for her and Zahara's livelihood, the judge would have the power to be lenient. She went and stood before the judge and explained all that she was doing: working (she might have had two jobs), going to school, maybe babysitting. The judge took leniency on her and granted her working papers or a green card. She impressed upon me how unusual it was for her to succeed in a career and to have taken care of herself. I think we shared something, obviously being Muslim. This idea of succeeding on your own without a family. I really appreciated that, and was amazed by her strength and perseverance."

"She hired a very expensive attorney to get her green card," Sue said. "For her to go through all of this, for a woman by herself and from where she was, and actually accomplish it, it was unbelievable."

"She had a lawyer in New York City who was doing the citizenship work," Debbie said. "He was not ethical. Nothing was moving along. He kept asking for more money and my stepdad, Uncle Don, was a lawyer, and they loved Nasrin, and he thought: 'This doesn't seem right, this should be happening faster,' so he made some phone calls or complaints to the bar. The next thing you know things started moving faster. And that became resolved and she became a citizen."

That was sometime in the 2000's – I remember Nasrin going to her ceremony in Buffalo.

"Ironically, in the end, Nasrin went through all the right channels and became a citizen before he did, if he ever did," Carolyn said. (According to other friends, Bahman divorced the wife in California, but it is unknown if he became a citizen).

"This is a woman and she's going to fight this," Debbie said. "Nasrin persevered. Good for her. She did not back down. She knew people who knew people. She was a very, very smart woman and knew how to navigate life. She was great. It didn't matter if we didn't see each other for a year, it was almost as if we knew each other in a different life. We always said: *God gave us each other*."

Life on West Hill, 1991- 1994

After Debbie moved to Michigan in 1991, Sue said, "Nasrin watched some twins on Hector Street in this little house that they rented. All I remember is the woman worked at Tops in the meat department."

When it became clear to her that her biology degree from Iran was worthless, Nasrin decided to go to Radiology School. But her English was not good. If she did have any English before emigrating, according to Carolyn, "It might not be very much. But she picked it up pretty quickly. Nasrin spoke the language of Mazandaran because she was from that province. She used to call it my *city language,* that was different from Farsi because she spoke two of them, plus English."

How did she learn to speak English?

"Practice," Debbie said. "My son, Jay, was very verbal. He could tell you stories about the love lives of others. And they watched *Sesame Street.*"

"She used to watch *Sesame Street* to learn," Sue said.

"By watching *Sesame Street* with them" (the children she babysat), Susan said.

"She always spoke English to me," Zahara said. "She said that she was trying to learn English herself and she was making herself speak English so she spoke it to me. She tried to teach me Farsi from a book."

"In a seemingly short time," Susan said, "she became sufficiently proficient in English to apply for an X-ray Technician program at T. Community Hospital and she got accepted on a scholarship. To become so adept at English, that she could understand medical terminology in a relatively short amount of time, I really think Nasrin had superior intelligence. She was academically intelligent and became socially and culturally intelligent very quickly. She had the determination and courage to preserve and make a good life for Zahara and herself."

"That would have been in the early '90s," Sue said. "She wanted to do something with her life. I don't think she was working while going to school, and for two years we opened our downstairs and family room. Bill offered two years for no rent. That worked out. The only thing was we could smell her food, and of course Laura would be downstairs sampling. She pretty much stayed down there. I guess we were more apt to go down there. Every day Zahara was going to the West Hill school to PreK, and she'd get off the bus and I'd stand at the sliding glass door so the driver knew I was there, and I'd have her after school so that helped Nasrin. Earlier she had helped me."

"I don't know why she decided to become an X-ray technician," Carolyn said. "She studied and did well, she was a smart woman, flying beneath the radar. If there was anything Nasrin had, it was determination. She suffered but she didn't give up, things did open up for her, but it wasn't as if she didn't work her butt off. She was quite inspiring in that way and look at the way she brought up Zahara – she was awesome, super-loving, but firm."

"The first part of my childhood she had absolutely no money and I have no idea how she made ends meet," Zahara said. "I found one of her tax returns from when I was three or four. She made $1,030."

At one point, Nasrin went to the Salvation Army for food, and took two loaves of bread. The volunteer there told her to put one back for someone else. Zahara: "She never wanted to feel that way again, it was a terrible moment, but it was the biggest motivator, and a blessing."

"She decided that she wanted to go to X-ray school because she wanted a better life than what babysitting was providing," Zahara said. "My guess is she probably talked to Sue about it because they were very close and Sue's husband worked at the hospital. I never asked her that. But she knew that the person who got the highest grades in the class would get a full scholarship, so she applied, and was not accepted. When she didn't get in, she found out where the admissions officer lived, the head of the program, and she went to his house, knocked on the door, introduced herself and said: 'This is so important for me. I really want a better life for my daughter and I promise you if you let me in, I'll get the highest grade in the class, and I will be your best student.' He said: 'We are full for this year, but you're in for next year.'

Then she lived up to that promise. She barely spoke English and was working and going to school and she somehow did really well."

"She was studying to take the exam for technician certification," Virginia said. "The first time she failed, but she persisted and did it again. It was hectic because she had to study, work, take care of Zahara, and she had little money."

"It was disappointing when we went to her graduation at the hospital. Nasrin had been the top student," Sue said. "Two other people were given these nice scholarships and they said they were the top students. Did they acknowledge her? No. She was upset about that."

Virginia met Nasrin at the CH Elementary School around 1992. Zahara had invited Virginia's daughter, Anita, to her birthday party. At that time, Virginia, Anita and her husband lived in West Village, a low-income apartment complex on West Hill. "We went to Cass Park with our daughters or she would come home for dinner or we would go to her place. She was busy and I was busy, so it wasn't as though we had a lot of time for ourselves. We did not have time to go out, for example, to have a cup of coffee. We did everything as a family so that our daughters could play together. Maybe it was the first year we met when she asked if I could look after Zahara during the summer because Zahara was out of school and Nasrin was working. Yes of course, I said. I was not working outside, I preferred to be at home, and babysitting was one thing I could do. After those two years of not being with my husband [Virginia needed to return to Argentina, her country of birth, to fulfill the requirements of a grant], I wanted to make the best of our place. I agreed with Nasrin on two or three dollars – something that she could afford and that helped me at the same time. It was mutually helpful." Virginia wasn't a *TV person* and she kept the girls busy with activities. Math and reading. "Nasrin would come and pick her (Zahara) up and we'd always talk – we'd open our hearts and say everything. No secrets. One day Nasrin came home with a pile of shirts that needed to have the collars fixed. She asked me if I would like to do this job (and get paid) with her, and I said *Sure!*"

Life on West Hill, Hook Place, 1994 -2003

Nasrin had been renting the upstairs of a house at the bottom of Hector Street, "Good sized, the biggest [space] we'd ever lived in," Zahara said. It was "pretty basic, but there was a yard, another kid" and they were happy. Then Nasrin bought her house on Hook Place. According to Sue, probably with some help from her family.

Zahara was seven or eight. The house was listed for $90,000 and in typical Nasrin-style, Nasrin offered $59,000, an offer that was surprisingly accepted. No doubt, when it came to financial transactions, Nasrin possessed magic. A small house on a steep hill, it always had water problems, and it lacked air-conditioning, but it was Nasrin's and Zahara's first home. "I don't remember any of them (Nasrin's friends) coming with us to look at houses," Zahara said. "She figured it out on her own. She liked West Hill because she had friends there."

The friends on West Hill at that time were Sue, Noni, Noni's Mom, Debbie (who left for Michigan), Virginia (who left later for Texas) and me (Pat) and all of our children.

"I vaguely remember the first time going over to her house on Hook Place," Anna said. Anna is representative of the younger generation who knew Nasrin. "I was in 4th grade. We had just moved to C. Heights school, I had been in Northeast school before, but I hadn't made any friends there and I was so excited when Zahara called me up to play. I remember being over there quite a bit, for sleepovers and birthday parties. We weren't friends in middle school – I don't remember why. But I ate there quite a bit. I don't remember that she cooked a lot of Iranian food – that started when I was older. She made more kid-friendly food for Zahara and her friends. Later on we had her Iranian food. It was really good."

"She also had a lot of friends who really liked her," Anna said. "She was good at sewing and she let me and Zahara pick out fabric. I picked out the ugliest fabric; in retrospect, that was the right response (not suggesting another fabric) and she sewed us pants. One for each of us so she must have made a lot of clothes for Zahara. There were the pajama pants. They were really cool, and not a small amount of work."

"We would have sleepovers at the house on Hook Place, and that was probably my first memory of Nasrin," April said. "The sleepovers: you know, we were in eighth grade so it was all very silly. A really interesting part of my relationship with Nasrin was seeing how it changed over time and as I grew up. At that time, she was very parental to everyone and extremely warm and the house always smelled like great Persian spices. It was very playful and free and there were a lot of different friends. Some houses were stricter than others, but her house was free-reign. And she seemed to trust us more than some parents. She was very extremely kind from the beginning."

"I do remember sleepovers," Hannah said. "One specific memory: Nasrin would make flan. I never had flan before and I thought it was the most amazing thing. Another memory: Zahara and I would always ask Nasrin to curl our hair with curlers and it would look absolutely terrible every time. Several times I would sleep over just to get her to do it, and it would never look quite like we thought it would. I remember going out in the morning after and having to hide our hair."

"I don't know how valuable my description will be but she was a stoic figure who was very formal and polite," Ben said. "But at the same time, she wasn't stuck up, and she'd be the sort of person that you could discuss complicated topics with, and she wouldn't just humor you, she would dive into them and be a good friend like that. She was in some ways a motherly icon. I would go to her house before school and she would give me all these little gifts. And it was always really nice and she would basically wait on us and she would let me watch TV. It was a cordial atmosphere, not upright or pretentious."

Anyone who went to Nasrin's house would be offered food. At the Hook Place house, she started a Thanksgiving tradition. According to Zahara: "She started celebrating Thanksgiving when I was in elementary school, and because she told my Dad, he tried to be nice and he ordered a turkey for us. It was really sweet of him but when we got to Wegman's they had already given away the turkey, and there were only pieces: legs, breast, and she was like *Oh my gosh, how embarrassing!* She had friends over, it didn't go as well as she had hoped, but she was an amazing host as you know, and so many Thanksgiving dinners after that."

She embraced other American holidays too. "She did celebrate Christmas," Zahara said. "She felt it was a nice tradition for children and she really got into it. She loved holidays and she also celebrated Easter and the Persian New Year, and that was the only Persian holiday she really held onto. I remember her fasting a few times on Ramadan. She was Muslim, and I went to a mosque with her in Iran. I never went to one with her here, there weren't any nearby. She was raised Muslim and she appreciated that side of herself."

Nasrin's Iran, 1992-2018

Nasrin returned to Iran several times for a month or so, the first trip being when Zahara was five years old, in 1992. Asked if her mom was hesitant to visit, Zahara said: "The relationship between the US and Iran was pretty good at that point and she really wanted to see her family. Before that the relationship was not good, and so she waited. And tickets were expensive. We both have Iranian passports, and my mother spoke Farsi, and that made it easier." As for returning to the US: "Sometimes they asked you a lot of questions, like what was the purpose of the trip, but the fact is, we have dual citizenship. Often, they [Iranians] will have you bribe them to let you through, but I think that happens to everyone. Once, when we were either going or coming back into the airport in Iran, they stole my birth certificate. They asked to see it and they wouldn't give it back to my mom."

"I'm sure she was scared to go back," Noni said, "that something would happen at the border, that she would have to stay."

"I know she loved going back to visit, I never heard her say she wanted to stay," Sorayya said. "But we did talk about how important it was to stay in touch with her mother and to visit. I was always interested in Iran, what it looked like to her, and in my imagination as well and while I was growing up in Pakistan when Iran was turbulent politically. What did the mountains look like? I had done some research for one of my novels about that and sometimes I would ask her."

"She knew things were not good [in Iran]," Sue said. "What she really wanted to do was bring all her family over here. Some got green cards. She worked hard to have them here. Her mother came once, but didn't want to come back. She did not like it here."

"We only talked about it [Iran] in terms of her family," Carole said. (Carole met Nasrin through her daughter, April, in the early 1990s). "She definitely had mixed feelings about her family. I feel she got along really well with her mom. She talked to her mom at least two or three times a week. She missed Iran, but she never really wanted to go back there to live, that was never in her plan. She liked it here."

"Nasrin wanted Zahara to know her family, especially her Grandmother," Susan said. "She wanted to take care of her Mom and bring her here. Family was important. She talked about her summer place on the Caspian Sea. I wish I had taken notes from every conversation we had about it because it would have been the most beautiful, rich book. The summer place, it sounded magical. When she was there, on her last trip to Iran, she sent me a picture of her and her Mom sitting at a picnic table."

"The warmth of the people really struck me," Zahara said, summing up her multiple visits to Iran. "They're all very, very open with their emotions and in a kind, loving and generous way that makes you feel welcome. That's something that my mom brought with her and that made her stand out in this culture. It's also more of a lively culture: there's lots of music and dancing, and get-togethers as people are always coming to each other's houses. You have more of family and community closeness than you do here. In certain areas of Iran, it's a very old-fashioned lifestyle in a sweet way: there are sheepherders and people who live in the mountains. They're disconnected from anything westernized and I would love Adam and Oliver to experience that. But it would be strange to go back without my Mom because she was the link to everybody in the family."

"Because she had her mother there," Zhila said. "She was a normal citizen. Even if I go back, this is information. Iran has information on all of us. They would know. They can take you even if they know your parents have done something. Nasrin lost her father. He was in business. I think the younger brother had a store – appliances – like *Bed, Bath and Beyond.* The older one was in real estate, and her sister's husband, jewelry. Her parents too, real estate. They never worked for the government so they are safe. They (Nasrin's brother and his family) come here every few months. They don't want to emigrate, but they want opportunities for their kids."

"My family is in California, and they don't want to leave," Zhila continued. "I can't imagine going back. Nasrin comes from a different city: it is green, near the water, from the north. I am from the capital. When I left, the population was three million, it is now 13 million. Our house was torn down and now there is a high rise. It is like Iliad turning into New York City. (Our entire county has a population of just over 100,000). Nasrin and I came here when we were students, 22, 23, if you ask me now to move to another country, it is impossible. My family is in Iliad. I like Iliad. I know my doctor. I cannot imagine going back to Iran. Iran is a different county."

"Once you are over nine-years-old," said Zahara, "as a female you have to be covered. I didn't like it, but it's a little thing. Covered from head to toe. Then you never know when you're walking down the street if you're going to get stopped by a police officer. They may ask you questions and so you definitely don't feel as safe or as comfortable and free as you do here. Other than that, you do have freedom to walk around and go wherever you want, you just have to abide by their rules." Asked if she would have felt comfortable on the streets by herself: "I don't speak the language, and I don't know the culture that well, and if I had been stopped by a police officer I don't think I would have been able to handle it in the right way. The police can be unpredictable: they can arrest you for no reason at all and hold you as long as they want."

Relations between the US and Iran have oscillated dramatically since the 1970's.

"My mom suggested not taking Adam and Oliver [to Iran] because they're not Iranian citizens. American citizens have been detained, so she recommended waiting to take them. My cousin recently became a US citizen. She was going to go back, but she's worried now that she's a US citizen, they might give her a hard time, so she's decided to wait."

"In person," Zahara said, "you can talk about it [the political situation]. When you're on the phone, the phone will often cut out if you start talking about politics. Or if you try to type anything, they monitor that as well."

"I have extended family there," Julia, Nasrin's second cousin who lives in Sweden, said. "My Mum and her family grew up there. I don't know much in terms of details. I've never been to Iran myself. My parents left during the Islamic Revolution. My dad had been very vocal and still is vocal against the regime. I have his surname and he could never go back. It's over-cautious and I worry – you never know what the regime would do with people who were vocal. I would love to go, just not with the current government."

"You never know what's going to happen in your country," Zhila said, "and it's surprising that it took [the Revolution]. Things got worse and the war. We all believed that the Khomeini rule would be temporary. Because of the potential for war and conscription, my niece and nephew were brought over. Eventually everyone started to come over. Iran was not a good place to go back to. They really didn't have any other choices. We came and worked very hard to get our degrees and jobs, and permanent residence, and it was not easy. Meanwhile the political situation in Iran did not get any better, people were living normal lives, but the political situation affected your life. My parents were affected. They sacrificed and sent money through the black market to ensure opportunities for their children and grandchildren. Our parents didn't want to come but eventually emigrated because they were lonely. They sold everything back in Iran and brought the money here. Now it is more difficult to bring money here. We knew we didn't want to go back. When you're not in a country for 35 years and there is a revolution, it is difficult. The regulations and laws for businesses have changed. We had to start from scratch."

Zhila's older son, who was in school with Zahara, "He went to Iran when he was eight for two months, but they never had the chance again: you're always concerned that if they go, because there is no American Embassy, and you are Iranian by the mother's blood, that no matter what, their mother is Iranian. Anything could happen to him. He could be easily drafted."

"My Mom did not talk much about the Iranian Revolution," Zahara said, "but it must have been a big part of her life. My Mom is someone who focuses on positive things."

"The US and Iran had a very good relationship with the Shah until 1978," Zhila said. "Then the military came to Iran, and because of financial transactions, the US relationship changed. Money was coming here, but without the product [probably military product] they could not even function. It was making everyone angry. There was a gap between the lower and middle class. Then the students took over the Embassy, and their ideology was close to that of Russia's. The US was very scared that Iran because we had so many resources. The US was afraid Russia would take over. The US government played a role for the Shah to leave. He lost his strength. Carter wouldn't let the Shah use arms against the students. There were so many students. It became a power vacuum. The government could not put the students in jail. And the students were close to Russia, so many kids close to that ideology. There was kind of a riot in Egypt, and the Shah went there. When the Shah left, Khomeini got power. We never had that in our history: basically a priest comes to power and takes over the government. No one thought it would last. After that I say anything is possible. We were saying: *Look at this type of people! Why those guys are like this?*"

Life on East Hill, 2004 to 2015

In 2004, wanting to be closer to work and Zahara's college, and frustrated with the Hook Place house's problems (mostly water invasion), Nasrin bought a house on East Hill from a doctor working at Guthrie Medical. It was half of a duplex, fairly new, dry and overall, in excellent condition.

Around this time, Nasrin's extended family, who had never been to the US, began visiting Nasrin for several weeks at a time. Because of US sanctions on goods, Iranian businesses were unable to acquire needed parts and supplies, forcing many small companies into bankruptcy. Nasrin's siblings believed their children would have more opportunity in the US and thus, their visits became longer and more frequent.

Consequently, Zahara was given ample opportunity to become acquainted with her extended Iranian family. "Iranians generally like Americans," she said. "Politics is often really different from your actual day-to-day cultural interactions between people. And things from the US are very highly regarded [in Iran]. If you brought back clothes or makeup or any sort of American product, they would be really excited, and they're always excited to come here. They're very welcoming people, and welcoming with people who aren't Persian."

Yet I wondered how did Iranians, other than through stated-owned media, acquire information about Americans? So I asked Zahara – maybe American life is depicted by American TV shows? "The TV is mostly Iranian, but you might be able to find American programs. Iranians still hear about pop culture in the US. But that might skew their vision of Americans and women. They might think that everyone lives glamorous lives. That's often something that I've heard from people who have moved here, that they thought life would be so glamorous and easy, and then they realize they have to work really hard. It's more like the pop culture that they get exposed to. Interacting with Americans doesn't happen as often; my cousins who live here know a lot about the music, so there must be a way that they're getting it. There are probably ways around the censorship."

Zahara graduated from high school in 2004 and in the fall attended college in Iliad, and lived in the dorms. Nasrin, who became Guthrie Medical's head radiologist in the 1990s, continued to work for Guthrie, five days-a-week, and often worked at the college nearby on the weekend. She always seemed to be working. When she and Zahara were living in poverty, there were no family visits; back then, her friends were her ballast, and there was always mutual admiration and emotional support. Nasrin's mother did visit in 2001 for several months, but did not speak English and was reluctant to leave the house much. Nasrin had mixed feelings about the visits from the extended family: she was happy to see them for a few days, but when the visits lasted months, it was hard on her. After working long days, she came home and cooked and cleaned. "It's the culture," she once told me. "It's expected."

Living with Cancer, 2016-2019

In February of 2016, while on winter layoff from my job, Nasrin asked me to take her to Guthrie Medical for a colonoscopy. A doctor who worked in the same building had ordered tests because he thought Nasrin "did not look well". Nasrin seemed weak: when I went for my yearly mammogram, she had difficulties lifting the X-ray plates and securing them. She commented on a weak shoulder, unusual for Nasrin. After the colonoscopy, we went back to Nasrin's house and watched a TV show. Nasrin had been given some preliminary results and she was in shock, but had not yet had a sit-down conversation with a doctor. She was deciding how and what to tell Zahara, although there was not yet much information, except that the doctor had found cancer.

According to Susan, "In Nasrin's case, they missed something, when Nasrin was coming out of the anesthesia she heard: 'This should have been caught on the last colonoscopy.' When she became fully conscious, not one owned up to the statement she'd heard."

"The doctor, also an incredibly close family friend, told me that they had discovered a malignant tumor during my mom's colonoscopy," Zahara said. "He assured me that it was stage one or two, and that it was treatable." At this time, Zahara and Adam were living and working in Boston, and left for Iliad when they got the news. At one point, when Zahara and Nasrin were alone, Nasrin said, "You don't have to pretend to be okay, you can tell me how you're really feeling." Zahara started to cry and admitted being scared. "She put her arms around me and told me that she was scared too. My mom knew how I felt, she understood me better than I understood myself. But I knew that what my mom feared most was having me feel pain."

"We stopped by her doctor's house a couple of days before her surgery," Zahara said, "and he causally mentioned that in her scan there had been a lymph node or two that had lit up. My mom seemed oblivious to what this meant, but I knew it was bad. Not early stage 1 or 2, but stage 3 and spreading. I held back tears and nausea. There was no reason to scare my mom."

"The night before the surgery, my mom had a horrible reaction to the pre-surgery medication. She ran to the bathroom to vomit, she didn't make it and I held her hair back as she threw up on the floor and in the sink. Seeing my mom so vulnerable and having to be the strong one assuring her that everything would be okay made me feel unsettled."

Nasrin had surgery on March 8, 2016. The doctor, according to Zahara, "assured her that the cancer was gone and she would be okay. A few days into her hospital stay, the surgeon came into her room. He asked me to sit down. I didn't understand why I was being asked to sit. He told us several lymph nodes were involved. It was staged as 3B. I asked him what the survival rate was. He said he didn't know the exact survival rates offhand, but I could come to his office. I followed him down a cement stairwell into a dark office and he took out his medical book. Forty-two percent. I was taken aback. 'You can't tell her this, it will destroy her.' The doctor agreed. He understood my mom well. I went back to my mom's room and painted an optimistic picture, saying that treatments had improved so much in recent years and people responded well to them. That night at my mom's home, I sobbed, and though my mom wasn't there, she called a friend to check on me, and I pretended to be fine, then went back to crying."

Zahara stayed with Nasrin, taking care of her after the surgery. The oncologist correctly typed Nasrin as "a special woman, that he needed to be kind and compassionate with her."

"A few weeks later my mom started chemotherapy. My mom needed 12 rounds of FOLFOX, each round lasted 50 hours and was given every other week. The first round didn't hit too hard, then the intense nausea, complete lack of energy and heart palpitations started."

"In the months that followed, I traveled back and forth from Boston to Iliad. When I wasn't around, her brother, sister or friends would be with her for treatments. They hit her hard: she often said it felt like her heart and brain were shaking and she sometimes had to crawl because she couldn't walk. Hair loss was not a usual side effect but my mom did lose a considerable amount of her hair. Despite feeling terrible, my mother went for a walk every day, even if it was slow and exhausting. Every treatment hit her with a wave of fear as she had to have blood work to show how her CEA tumor markers were progressing, and how her organs were functioning. I felt her fear. The CEA levels looked promising though: originally at 78 before surgery, they dropped to 7 and then fell below 3 during chemotherapy. Lower than 3 is considered a normal CEA level."

Nasrin, who worked in the health field, was very aware of stress and its impact on the mind and body and was keen on trying meditation, which she did. According to Headspace[3] "Meditation has been scientifically proven to help alleviate stress just after eight weeks of a regular practice. Meditation ultimately reprograms the brain to the extent that meditators end up with more capacity to manage stress." At one point in 2016, I took Nasrin for another procedure in Pennsylvania. I don't remember what we talked about on the drive south – probably our kids – anything but her health.

When we got to the hospital, it was dark outside. Most of the hospital was empty. There were no greeters with maps at the front desk. Even the lights seemed less bright. I bought some pretzels and we ate the entire bag, then we sat on plastic chairs in an empty hallway. We waited. I had my phone and earbuds and I gave Nasrin one bud, and I took the other and we listened to a meditation. Most of it was a silent meditation. And that was okay.

Zahara and Adam planned for a wedding in July 2016; Zahara wanted to postpone it, but Nasrin nixed that idea and refused to give up her role as seamstress, and made both her dress and Zahara's. "The week before my wedding my mom's platelet levels dropped too low to continue that round of treatment. This was a blessing in disguise, having one treatment three weeks since her last chemotherapy session, my mom was able to enjoy the wedding."

"We woke up early on July 23, 2016, and decided together we would fix the disastrous bouquets from the florist. We cut down a good amount of my mom's garden. This felt like the us that we used to be: best friends finding joy in tackling life's little challenges together. My mom walked me down the aisle, which was fitting as she had raised me. At the reception she danced the night away and had endless energy. She always said that that was the best day of her life. For me, the best part of my wedding was seeing my mother's happiness."

Zahara and Adam were married – by Carolyn – in an elegant church on the university's campus. The reception took place at a winery with spectacular views to C. Lake. There was tasty food, Iranian cookies, a bar, a deejay, and an expansive dance floor. The July night was perfect: warm, clear and sunny until sunset. Everyone seemed radiant.

"My mom started her next round of chemotherapy the day before Adam and I left for our honeymoon." Nasrin continued with the chemotherapy, lowering the dose when her platelet levels were not high enough. The last treatment was in September. "They had her ring a bell signaling the end of her journey and the beginning of remission. She cried, as did the nurse. I felt numb."

Zahara found out she was pregnant a few days before Thanksgiving in 2016, and wanting to tell her mom in person, she kept this secret for three days. "[It] was so difficult, we talked every day for an hour and shared every detail of ours lives. My mom's greatest dream was to have grandchildren." This Nasrin conveyed to Zahara when she was a few years old. Once back in Iliad, Zahara gave her mom a present of white baby booties. "As she opened the box, she let out a gasp: I had never seen my mother so overcome by shock and excitement."

Still Nasrin had not been "herself since her diagnosis"; she was "someone different probably because of fear and her anti-anxiety medication. I felt like I had already lost a part of my mom. Our phone conversations now involved her seeming to be checked out, and saying, "what else" in response to everything I said. I needed my mom but the mom that I once knew was no longer available. At times I felt it was a blessing: losing pieces of her slowly instead of all at once."

At Nasrin's three-month follow-up, six weeks after Oliver was born, because of increased CEA tumor markers, and results from CT and PET scans, Nasrin had surgery in late September 2017. Zahara was in Boston. After the surgery, Nasrin called with optimism to report three cancerous spots, believing them to be "left over from the original surgery and not systemic spread." According to Zahara: "Metastasis to the abdominal cavity has 0-5% year survival with a 6- to 9-month average survival, without chemotherapy." Chemotherapy would have added a couple of months of life.

Nasrin was adamant about no more chemo. She mentioned uncontrollable shaking and nausea, and when I suggested she stay at my house, she declined. She eventually moved to Boston and lived with Zahara, Adam and Oliver. They started researching the natural approaches to cancer, such as eating a raw vegan diet "coupled with fresh vegetable juicing and emotional healing." Nasrin started the diet in October and allowed herself one cooked dish a week. "Broccoli," she told me. "After three weeks, you get used to it."

"It pains me to say this," Zahara said, "but she always seemed to be dragging her feet, complaining about the juice and salads. She was terrified to eat anything. I told her the diet was meant to empower her and heal her body, nothing about it was going to harm her. But this plan only seemed to reinforce her fear of food. She would ask me for permission to eat almost anything and get frustrated when I said she could eat whatever she wanted. I believe it was her state of mind, and I pushed her to let out her emotions. I tried everything I could, but she was incredibly resistant and it started to feel like she loved me, but she no longer liked me."

"And I needed my mom."

The next year life changed, as if often does, and for most of 2018 Nasrin became Oliver's second Mom. "He was the only thing that truly brought her joy," Zahara said. She took care of Oliver during the day while Zahara and Adam worked. "We traveled as a family to Toronto and London. She also traveled to Iran."

She came to Julia's and Shiv's wedding in London. "My husband and I are oncologists and we spoke to her about whether she should be pursuing more aggressive chemo, and I know she was very adamant, she wanted to pursue alternative therapy. We initially disagreed: this is not a wise choice at the time. She ended up having a really good year of life. She was very happy, she had hope, and that hope gives you life. Had she been on chemotherapy to extend her life – for two months? Is it worth it if it means vomiting and not feeling so well? Her experience definitely changed my views around death and palliative care and things like that, and the vulnerability of life."

Shiv: "I gave her my opinion which she disagreed with. And to tell the truth, it completely changed the way I thought about a lot of it, because you do what you think is in her best interest, but she didn't want to go ahead with the chemo, and actually the condition she had was terminal. She declined, and that surprised me, and she gave me a reason: she wouldn't be able to do what she wanted, and she actually wanted to come to our wedding, the year before she died. And up until the last few weeks she actually had a good quality of life. She was very happy to travel. The flight to London, which is quite a long journey, and then she was engaged in all aspects of our wedding and that really taught me something."

"What was remarkable about Nasrin," Marie said (she met Nasrin on the East Hill walking trail), "was that through her illness and pain, even when hanging on by a thread, she would ask me: 'How are *you* doing?' One of the last things she said to me was that she wanted to cook for me. Up to the end, she was always thinking of others. When she asked, 'How are you?' she had a way of looking at you deeply in the eyes, unhurried, and sincerely wanting to connect at a deeper heart level."

"The last two times she went to Iran," Carole said, "she visited a spiritual (leader), not a guru. Several times. He told her to do some spiritual activities, and honestly, I don't remember what those were. He told her she was going to get well, and she hung onto those words."

I recall Nasrin sending her medical files to doctors in Iran, and the doctors chastising her for pursuing medical treatments in the US, and also assuring her that she would get well.

"At one point," Carole said, "we were trying to get her to consider Roswell Cancer Center in Buffalo. She just said no. It was hard. She did not want to pursue chemo again."

Still Nasrin walked nearly every day and took up running for the first time. In fact, Nasrin ran the Turkey Trot with me on Thanksgiving Day in 2018. While in Iran, however, she started having stomach pains and discovered a lump in her abdomen.

"In mid-December, she had been watching Oliver all day, full of energy as usual, and in the evening she said she felt off and went upstairs to lay down. I found her lying on the floor barely able to talk or move. She insisted she just needed some rest. When I closed the door to her room that night, I did not know if she would be alive in the morning."

The next day, a day that terrified everyone, Zahara and Adam took Nasrin to ER, and they were told the cancer was blocking her liver. "We went home with a referral to palliative care." In Boston, Nasrin became sicker and sicker, "an odor permeated her room that smelled like death and decay." They decided to drive back to Iliad, stopping multiple times to allow Nasrin to vomit.

"Christmas and New Years were spent in the hospital." There were five more surgeries, including one to insert stents in her bile ducts and to bypass a blockage in her small intestine. "I held my mom's hand as a very kind doctor told her that her cancer was everywhere. She insisted she wasn't giving up, and now had the will to live even more." In January, she was back in the hospital for a blood infusion and treatment for an infection.

"In January I went with her to have a tube replaced," Susan said. She took the doctor aside and asked him: "'Do patients live long after this?' 'No,' he said. Driving home, I felt this unsurmountable gap between us. How do you make the decision to bring up the issue of death? I felt that it would draw energy from her, and that was all she had. I didn't want to say anything that would shake her confidence, what little she had left to navigate life with. When someone has everything taken away from them, you don't want them to lose hope. I wasn't going to talk about death."

I felt similarly, as did many of her friends.

Nasrin continued to lose weight, was in pain, and had trouble sleeping. "After having trouble breathing, Hospicare brought in an oxygen tank; although my mom fought hard against morphine, she gave in after a night of pain that was beyond anything she had ever felt." I remember Nasrin texting me: "It's okay to take morphine?" "Absolutely," I texted back. "Yes, you can get off of it," I told her, although it wasn't likely. I am sure she consulted her other "sisters" on this issue.

"My mom was my whole world, my best friend. I needed support. My mom was too overwhelmed to comfort me and my own friends had never been through anything close to this and wanted to be supportive but didn't know how. My mom's friends were amazing, they visited every day, made food, sat with her, and cared for her. Susan [Nasrin's dearest friend and a nurse] spent hours every night helping my mom get comfortable and sitting and talking with her." Hospicare helped with advice, and an aide came to the house every morning.

"My mom's Hospicare nurse sat me down and told me my mom only had days left. She cried with me. Despite my mother insisting that she would get better and being on the brink of death for months, she somehow sensed it was the end. She sat me down and told me she wanted me to be happy. She wanted Oliver and Adam to be happy. And when I started to cry, she said, 'Hey, don't be sad. I'm still here!' And we both laughed, she still had a way of making everything okay."

"I was in the room when Nasrin died," Zhila said. "Zahara kissed her and cried. I have never had that experience. Hospicare came that day and said it would be soon. She died at 7:30 p.m.. She suffered, and was resistant to death. Finally she said, 'Zahara, could you bring me some morphine?' I never saw any child love her mother this much. Mine never would. Zahara was in a very bad situation, but she was protected by Adam. She got the best person in her life. I never thought I would be able to do it. I closed Nasrin's eyes. Hashem's wife was there to cover her. Zahara said to get rid of all the medicine. We did. Then we called Hospicare."

"Obviously we know that cerebrally," Marie said, of life and death. "It's strange and unsettling to see a person regularly and then suddenly they are no longer there. In Nasrin's case, I was there as she passed, and as I knelt by her body, I could actually feel her being, her presence still there, but unattached to her body. I've experienced this with animals but it was the first time that I experienced this with a person. What I know is that life continues on, and I know this sounds like a cliché, but we are never separate after being connected with someone."

"The last picture I have of her," Susan said, "was when I came in the room. Usually I moved her. I was surprised that she was sitting straight up. Her eyes were closed and she seemed comfortable. I went home to get dinner, then her niece called and I raced back. There was a sheet pulled over her head, and I said, 'I need a minute.' Marie sprinkled rose petals, and I thought, okay, I can deal with this. People went out. Her eyes were open, and what you have to do within the first hour, rigor mortis, you want the eyes closed. I closed the right and

Marie closed the left. And we put the sheet over her. I remember a scream, Zahara crying, and then taking Oliver into her room with Adam. Then two young funeral guys came in. Zahara didn't want Oliver to run out. At one point, Oliver did get out. In 20 minutes, they brought out her body in a body bag, a gym bag really. Holy moly, I thought: this is what your life comes to!"

"Zhila was there and Nasrin's sister: who wants to have lots of people?" Susan said. "But that was the way she grew up, Nasrin was used to having lots of people over. Another friend remarked: 'This is awful, all these people,' and I thought: You can't take over! But at the same time, I would want one person at a time, not four or five. I asked Zhila about her last moments. 'Breathing came calmly, then inhale and no exhale.' That was it. I gave her her last morphine at 4:30. I asked if she was feeling pain, and ever so slightly, with the shake of her head, she would tell me. Morphine makes breathing easier, but it has a depressive effect. It's a mind blower when a human being dies. You try to understand, but it's all a big joke in a way, it's not all that serious: one moment you're there and the next you're gone. It's an energy drain, that is the main component of dying: a deep, deep energy drain."

Part II: Immigrants, Immigration and Iran

Immigrants

I began writing this section on immigrants while visiting Anna, my daughter, in Jena, Germany, February 2020. Down the road from 57 Middlestrasse where Anna lives, at 36 Middlestrasse is a pair of stumbling stones, or stolpersteine, Holocaust monuments. The brass "stones", 10 cm by 10 cm, embedded in the sidewalk, bear the names, birth dates, deportation date, concentration camp and death of the individual/family who once lived at that address. During the war forty Jews from Jena were deported to camps such as Buchenwald, Auschwitz, and Mauthausen. January 27, 2020, marked the 75th anniversary of the liberation of Auschwitz. Last year when Anna and I were plotting out our European itinerary, I suggested visiting Poland. *Too much anti-Semitism*, she said. Having grandparents that survived the Holocaust has made Anna more keenly aware of anti-Semitism. Anna has lived in Jena for nearly three years but initially had misgivings: how would she be perceived? So far, she has made many good, close German friends. I asked her how many other Jews she had met in Jena. *One.*

Over 98 percent of Americans were once immigrants; only 2% of the American population can claim to be of Native American descent.[1] The majority of Americans were immigrants at one time, yet we have a history of marginalizing, ghettoizing and persecuting immigrants. We used to be known as the great "melting pot experiment" where people from different ethnicities lived somewhat harmoniously, side-by-side, or at least, that's what the schools in the 60s taught us. I don't know how true this is anymore; in some places in the US certainly, but not in others. With some cultures and ethnicities certainly, but not with others. In Iliad, I recently saw a bumper sticker that made me smile: *We are a nation of immigrants, not ignorance.* But I have also seen confederate flags, and Nasrin, when she was house-hunting, once told me about a Nazi enclave out on route 79. (Verified by the rabbi at Temple Beth El: *Yes, it's there*, he said, matter-of-factly.) Although biracial marriages these days rarely get an eye blink (depending where in the US you are), the prison industrial complex would disappear were it not for the minorities it incarcerates.

Immigrants, the poor, and those just starting out in life, do the hardest, most dangerous and most unappealing work in any country: construction, farm work, meat processing. I remember briefly picking strawberries before I was old enough for working papers. You don't make a lot of money picking strawberries. Immigrants have to work harder to get ahead, especially when you don't understand the culture or the unwritten rules, or lack a job network and the support of a nearby family.

We know that America is a stronger country because of immigrants. Immigrants are the backbone of the country. They bring new ideas, practices, skills, foods, culture. You name it. In "The Open Borders Trap,"[2] Jason Deparle said we don't often make the case that immigration "strengthens the economy, invigorates the culture and deepens ties to the world" and instead focus on food and daycare. "I once asked a leading scholar of immigration what benefits it had brought America, beyond good food and affordable day care. *Don't underestimate the value of good food and child care,* the scholar replied."

Justin Malik says "Interacting with people who are different to us – whether in terms of culture, views, or age – is good for us. It makes our lives richer and our minds sharper."[3] Which makes one wonder: if we had understood the people of Iran, would the 1979 Hostage Crisis have occurred?

Immigration

Immigration has become a contested topic all over the world. War and unstable governments, governments that severely restrict an individual's rights make living in those countries untenable which produces immigrants. It's a huge topic in America at the moment, and huge in Germany. Last week (February 2020) in Jena university students were protesting the power given to a far-right candidate. Anna and I passed by this anti-fascist rally after lunch. It was a Saturday and there was a crowd of 200 or 300. Of the speaker, Anna said, "He is demanding that the elected leader whose party made a secret coalition with the Far-Right step down." There were some anti-fascist signs, and graffiti on many buildings, most of it in German so its intent was unknowable to me. Yet Anna assured me that Jena, which is a little larger than Iliad, is a university town, and its people, educated. Germany, population nearly 90 million, in an effort to resolve some of its past, has opened its doors to Syrian refugees. Online information indicates around 600,000 Syrians living in Germany. By comparison, the US, in 2016, allowed in fewer than 13,000 immigrants. Still, not all Germans welcome the refugees.

Sonia Nazario in a *New York Times* article,[4] "gives some clarity to the immigration issue. Nazario's mom was a Jew who fled Poland; her dad, a Christian Syrian. There is currently a bill before the Senate, *Refugee Protection Act*, which would allow in at least 100,000 immigrants just from El Salvador, Guatemala and Honduras. "Well, our laws say we have to help people who are running for their lives," Nazario says. "Take it from a Nazario: President Trump is the one who has broken the law."

Nasrin worked hard for her American citizenship. I remember her telling me, proudly, that she was going to Buffalo for her ceremony. I'm sure she knew facts about the country that I did not. American citizenship gave her more opportunity and stability in a country that to our non-credit, has become increasingly hostile towards immigrants. For me and certainly everyone I have interviewed for this book, our lives would be less interesting, not nearly as warm or rich without our friendship with Nasrin.

An Italian friend of mine, who is married to an immigrant from the Dominican Republic, stated that the best way to break down racial barriers, other than interracial marriage, is to have close friends from other ethnicities.

A colleague at work, a young man in his 30s who has become a good friend, said: "Most of us don't think about who is black, white or brown. Maybe that's our generation." True, but there also seems to be an upsurge of White Supremacist, anti-immigrant and anti-Semitic activity in many countries, including the US. In response, there has been a proliferation of books that probe deeper into the American culture, and as they do, they dislodge myths and educate white people about the meaning and costs of institutional racism. Some of the more well-known books, which the younger generation had recommended, and I have read, are Ibram X. Kendi's *How to be an Antiracist* and Michelle Alexander's *The New Jim Crow*.

When Nasrin and I talked about politics it was always in person. Never over the phone, never by text, and never in an e-mail. It was too dangerous for her: in the back of her mind, the fear of deportation was real. And what of her experiences with racism, in an exceptionally diverse and educated community like Iliad? There was a handyman who remodeled Nasrin's garage into an apartment. He swindled her out of two thousand dollars and the Court refused to hear her case. Because she was a woman, or an immigrant? But Nasrin understood that to spend time on negative people was to waste her life. She even warned me once about a former boyfriend: *Your boyfriend is too negative and you will use all of your energy fighting him.*

Nasrin, who eventually became the head radiographer at Guthrie Medical (from a babysitter with no English to head radiographer!), was teaching a new hire, Valerie, the system, when Valerie got into a terrible car accident. That year Valerie and her family came to Nasrin's

Thanksgiving dinner. *Who are these people,* I wondered? As Valerie recuperated, Nasrin, in typical style, held Valerie's job open for her. Valerie no sooner returned to work than she became a harassing presence in Nasrin's life. "She would undermine Nasrin," Susan said. Susan worked for several years as a nurse at Guthrie Medical. "She would sit and read her Bible and ignore her job." Like anyone, it frustrated Nasrin to be treated unfairly, but unlike most, she persevered. She worked harder.

There were other unattractive incidents at Guthrie, yet there were people who protected her. During my last mammogram with Nasrin in 2016, she was having a hard time lifting the X-ray plates. A Guthrie doctor took her aside claiming she didn't look well, and ordered some tests for her, including a colonoscopy.

Anna and I are on the train from Zagreb to Slovenia. In Zagreb we went to several bookstores because we wanted to get a sense of the Bosnian War, the war of ethnic cleansing that occurred in the Balkans in the 1990's. Before the trip, I had a hard time placing Croatia on the globe. Now I am familiar with its location: south of Hungary (birthplace of Anna's grandfather), east and south of Slovenia and the other Balkan countries: Bosnia and Herzegovina, Serbia, Montenegro and Macedonia. We started reading Noam Chomsky's *Yugoslavia, Peace, War and Dissolution.*[5] Josip Broz Tito, president of the Socialist Federal Republic of Yugoslavia for 27 years, somewhat successfully kept the Balkan countries united. He died in 1980, leaving behind a Yugoslavia that was economically failing, that would become fractured and eventually dissolve. Yugoslavia had "six federal republics, two autonomous provinces, three religious groups," and many ethnic groups: Albanians, Hungarians, Romanians, Bulgarians, Serbs, Croats, Muslims, Slovenians, etc. The brutal and violent battle for territory, resources, and power left about 100,000 dead).[6] Some leaders (Milošević) were tried and convicted of genocide.

At the border of Croatia and Slovenia, as we cross into Slovenia, several police with dark navy flack vests enter the nearly empty train, examine our passports, then scan them electronically. Other police search underneath the train's wheels with flashlights. A few feet from where we sit, another unscrews an overhead panel, and probes the tiny spaces with his flashlight.

Iranians in the US

Iranian or Persian? Nasrin would call herself a Persian, however since 1935 the term Iranian-American has been used, as well as Persian-American; since 1959, Persia has also been referred to as Iran.[7] Most of this chapter is based on this Wikipedia article; exceptions are noted. Most Iranians are of Persian descent, but not all; minorities include Kurds and Azeris. There are also Assyrians and Armenians, which are Christian minorities, the Assyrians indigenous to Northwestern Iran, Azerbaijan Province.[8]

It may come as no surprise to those who have Iranian friends, that Iranians are highly educated, and have "historically excelled in business, academia, science, the arts, and entertainment." There is no country that has more Iranian immigrants than the US. Most Iranians emigrating to the US settle in California, mostly in Los Angeles, in the neighborhood known as Tehrangeles.

Iranians first emigrated to the US in the late 40's, eager to attend the US's colleges and universities. By 1975 Iranian students made up the largest group of foreign students in the US. Universities welcomed Iranian students: they knew English and they were intelligent and hard-working. Iran had the ability to send students abroad given sky-rocketing oil prices in the 1970s that translated into a strong and growing Iranian economy.

From 1975 to 1977, the number of Iranian visitors in the US more than doubled, from 35,000 to 98,000. The 1979 Revolution, which established the Islamic Republic of Iran, essentially made existing students refugees; those who returned to Iran were "purged" or in danger of being "purged"; thus, students were not keen on returning to their country. Because of this "brain-drain," Iran lost many of its best minds. How Iranian students were treated in the US is another matter, and is described in another section of this book, The 1979 Hostage Crisis.

Another phase of immigration, this one of well-off professionals, occurred during the 1980-1988 War with Iraq. Because a "considerable amount of wealth" left the country, Iran was transformed "politically, socially and economically." The US obviously benefited from this immigration.

Data from 1980 US Census indicated 123,000 Americans of Iranian ancestry were living in the US; this number increased by 74 percent by 1990. From 1995 to the present (2020), represents the third phase of Iranian immigration. One estimate (2011) indicates 470,300 "Americans with full or partial Iranian ancestry" live here, but other estimates of one million-plus may be more accurate.

Amol, Mazandaran Province, Iran

Nasrin often mentioned that her city of birth was Amol, but I never knew much about the city. Endeavoring to deepen my understanding of Iran and Iranians, I found some information online.[9-11] Thus descriptions are neither broad nor conclusive, and I invite anyone with additional information to contact me. I regret not asking Nasrin more about where she grew up, and what her life was like then.

Amol is a city in Mazandaran Province in northern Iran. The city sits on the Haraz river, 12 miles from the Caspian Sea, and as such is an important port. It's about six miles from the Alborz mountains, and 110 miles from Tehran. The province's plains stretch to Mount Damavand, which at 5,610 meters, is the highest peak in the Middle East.

Amol was founded in 224 as a Nestorian Christian episcopate, and since its founding has experienced invasion and ransacking by enemies in the 11th and 14th centuries, and periodically, just to add to the general distress, earthquakes and floods.

The city appears as a cityscape of moderately-high, somewhat uniform apartments. Beyond the city center are forests, verdant pastures, valleys, thermal springs and waterfalls. If you visit unsplash.com,[12] you will find photos that include these scenes: mountains, a vast field of yellow flowers, a sea-side camp, trees and leaves, a young attractive woman who bears a surprising resemblance to Zahara, two legs sticking out of a body of water, an outdoor food market, a mosque and a high rise, a cat sauntering across an ornate floor, a gorgeous mountain sunset, fireworks, food, waterfalls, a dog on a hilltop and a painting of a *man riding on a levitation broom*. Nasrin often talked about her summer house in the mountains, and I imagine some of these photos represent her small piece of heaven on earth, but Nasrin would add: with a climate milder than central New York's.

Amol's current population is around 240,000, or about the size of Madison, Wisconsin, still a small city. Most Amoli speak the Mazandarani language, or Tabari; however, Persian or Farsi is the national language. At present, the majority of people are followers of Shia Islam. Most of the existing schools, roads and governmental buildings were built by Reza Shah Pahlavi, who ruled Iran from 1925 to 1941. The Islamic Azad University, one of the largest universities in the Middle East, is in Amol, and contributes to Amol's reputation as a scholarly center. Several leaders of the Iranian constitutional revolutions of 1905 and 1911 hailed from Amol. In 1982 there was *The Jungle Uprising,* where the Union of Iranian Communists (Sarbedaran) waged wars against the Iranian government. The organizers failed, and they were hanged.

Amol produces wooden artifacts, carpets, and textiles—the silks being especially famous. You would walk into Nasrin's house and think: this is definitely not an American house as your eyes settled on the gold, rust, and warm brown-colored fabrics, the tablecloths or pillow covers with transparent beads and mica carefully sewn into the fabric.

Today Amol is a tourism draw – just look at the photos – who wouldn't want to travel there? It's an agricultural center and exports minerals, livestock and dairy products to Russia, the US (surprise!), Iraq, Germany, Pakistan, Saudi Arabia, Turkey, Angola, Oman, United Arab Emirates and Azerbaijan.

Amol, known as *The City of Mystics and Philosophers*, is a center for Iranian culture and has produced famous poets. Apparently Amoli people enjoy books, clothes and food. They go to movies, art exhibitions, concerts and book fairs. Sounds a bit like Iliadians. I would imagine that if you could avoid the morality police, and if its policies did not affect your livelihood or state of mind, then Amol would be a very nice place to live.

Why didn't Nasrin talk more about Amol? One can only speculate. That she loved the city and Iran is clear, but after Iran became the Islamic Republic of Iran in November 1979, all of Iran changed, and not in ways that allowed women their independence or integrity. And there was this penchant of Nasrin's to move ahead, always move on to the next challenge. She wasn't about to dwell on what she lost, even something very dear to her.

Iran: The Past

To understand Nasrin' life, it seemed incumbent to include a brief description and some history on Iran. Zhila, another friend of Nasrin's and also Iranian, recommended William Polk's book, *Understanding Iran*.[13] William Polk, an American who was directly involved in the politics of Iran for many years, wrote: "Iran has had one of the world's richest and most fascinating historical experiences. One should ask: how much of it is pertinent today? Do Iranians today really remember their past over the last 2,000 or so years? Or is this book just a historian's contrived assemblage of events?" Read on if you have an interest in an answer to his questions and desire more knowledge about Persia/Iran, and from an author who loves the country and the people. The quotes are from Polk's book, unless stated otherwise.

A quick glance at a globe or the map included near the book's beginning indicates Iran's complicated geographical and political location: Kuwait and Iraq to the west, then going north, Turkey, Armenia, Azerbaijan, the Caspian Sea, Turkmenistan to the north and east, and going further east, Afghanistan and Pakistan, and southward, the Gulf of Oman, the Straits of Hormuz, the Persian Gulf. Of course Iran's (Persia's) borders have changed throughout the past 2,000 years. A closer look at the country indicates that most of central Iran is made-up of deserts – the Kavir and Lut deserts being the largest. A tourist website[14] that identifies Iran's deserts states: "The ecological conditions of Deserts of Iran are so severe in a way that they are not tolerable either in summer or winter." Interesting publicity from a tourist site.

To the west are the Zagros Mountains, to the north, the Alborz or Elbruz Mountains. Nasrin's city, Amol, is near the Alborz Mountain chain. Listings of the smaller mountains and these ranges along with photos can be found at a Wikipedia site[15]. Iran's highest peak, Mount Damavand (5,610 meters), is found in Manzandaran Province, where Nasrin lived. Mount Damavand is also the highest volcano – stratovolcano, because of its conical shape, built-up from layers of ash, tephra and pumice – and erupted last in 5,300 BC. Because of its fumaroles, which emit sulfuric gases, Mount Damavand is classified as a potentially active volcano. Associated with the fumaroles are mineral hot springs which draw the recreational crowd.[16]

"A notable feature of Iran today," Polk states, "is that in 1909 an oil field was brought into production near the Persian Gulf. Large gas reserves were subsequently found and developed nearby. Plentiful and usually cheap Iranian energy has played a major role in the industrialization of the European developed world . . . [But] the way these resources were developed was often skewed to fit the world market rather than the needs of the country, and often was a cause of disruption and discontent rather than support and security for Iran."

If you dig deeper into Persia, which was not referred to as Iran until 1935, you'd find underground canals – ghanats. Lack of water is a deciding factor in a country with major deserts and little rainfall. You'll discover a country beset throughout its history with power struggles, countries appealing to other countries for protection, extreme poverty, and a great intermingling of diverse people, disease (small pox), enticements of sex, opium and liquor, importation of slaves, protests and revolutions, wars with neighboring countries, wars with distant countries like Greece, and in particular Macedonia. Alexander The Great (356-323 BC), a Macedonian: "crashed through the Persian Empire: from Egypt, through Syria to Iraq, on to Central Asia and Afghanistan and down to India, he chased the Persian ruler and destroyed his armies. He killed off the royal family, disrupted the bureaucracy and suppressed the "church" that had held the Persian Empire together, razing Zoroastrian temples, massacring the Zoroastrian priests."

But there were also years of peace. Certain empires (Sasanian) "brought together diverse elements that were enjoyed by a rich and refined society in security and peace." Ancient Persia welcomed Nestorian Christians and other philosophers. According to Polk: "A recurrent theme in history – the seeking of sanctuary and the quest for education, in our times, have brought tens of thousands of Iraqis into Iran." But a mixture of people and cultures – Persians, Turks, Mongols, Arabs, Europeans, and religions: Judaism, Christianity, Zoroastrianism, Islam – created power struggles and cultural and social clashes. Still, education was important to Persians. This was a mission for the Seljuks – a group of tribes – who conquered eastern Iran in 1040. The Seljuk Prime Minister, a Persian named Nizam ul-Mulk: "Created the most impressive education systems in the world of his time. He aimed to establish a college of higher learning in every significant city in the Seljuk Empire; he planted in the minds of successive rulers down to our own times an ideal of government that could be measured by its dedication to education."

Persia suffered greatly from the invasion of Genghis Khan in 1215, and future invasions in 1258 by Mongol armies that ransacked cities, destroyed vital irrigation systems, and murdered craftsmen. "Their policy aimed to convert the agricultural lands to the open pasture the nomads wanted, and they carried it out by genocide. Most of the famous old cities of Iran were virtually annihilated by attack after attack; in the wake of the armies came famine and pestilence. Cities shrank into towns and towns shrank into villages. Many villages simply disappeared." Polk states that the memory of this "horrifying experience planted in the collective memory of Iranians an abiding fear of foreign invasion. The effects linger to this day."

A closer study of Iran's geography reveals small rivers in the west and north, but no large major river; such rivers, before the trains and highways appeared, were crucial transportation and trading routes. Because of its lack of major rivers, travel in Iran was often "difficult and always expensive" and isolation was common. According to Polk its cities "developed distinctive local cultures. European visitors were sometimes charmed, and often infuriated by the Iranians they met. Foreigners found the Iranians exotic and bizarre, but sometimes enchanting." From an English merchant (1561): the Persians were "comely and of good complexion, proude and of good courage, esteeming themselves to bee best of all nations, both for their religion and houlinesse, which is most erroreous, and also for other their fashions. They be martial, delighting in faire horses and good harnesse,

Iran: The Present

We have had no formal diplomatic relations with Iran since 1979. Because my college training was in the sciences, none of my classes ever mentioned Iran except in a broad geological context, and in relation to petroleum exploration. From my high school history classes, I don't recall much about the Middle East: I attended a Catholic high school in Buffalo, and most of my classes were taught by nuns, who were not exceptionally worldly. I have been to Canada, Mexico, Europe, Israel, Zimbabwe and South Africa, but I have never traveled to the Middle East which sadly, reinforces my ignorance and lack of awareness of the region and its people. I knew nothing about Iran until 1979, when the Hostage Crisis erupted. This event was a monumental source of frustration and anxiety for both countries.

Occasionally there are newspaper articles about Iran, mostly about how the theocracy oppresses its citizens or violates an international arms agreement, and the consequent US sanctions which are disastrous to the Iranian people. Nasrin often mentioned her relatives' businesses failing because they could not get parts, forcing many to emigrate. Most certainly the news we read about Iran is one-sided and casts the country in an unfavorable light. Most of the news is not about people.

There was an incident in the summer of 2009 where three Americans hiking near the Iraq-Iran border were taken by Iranian border guards and imprisoned for over a year, and this cemented our perception that the Iranian government was irrational and paranoid. Iran alleged that the hikers who stepped onto Iranian territory were spies, not three young American teachers hiking in the mountains and enjoying nature. But this is our perception of Iran: a country that takes hostages. And their impression of us: the magical country where consumerism and freedom for women plays too heavy a role in life.

The current president of Iran, elected in 2013, Hassan Rouhani[17] ran on a platform of "recalibrating Iran's relations with the world". He promised greater political and social freedom and nuclear transparency. However, opposing forces have accused him of being "infected by Western doctrine" and it's not clear how much power Rouhani has.

During his first 14 months as president, he executed almost 600 people. Although a supporter of women's rights, he may not have the power to institute changes to promote women's rights. Reportedly censorship of the internet has become more severe under his leadership. In 2013 Rouhani released 11 political prisoners, but this was days before a meeting at the United Nations General Assembly. At that time, he declared to the Obama Administration (phone call to Obama) a willingness to establish relations with the US However, this led to a chorus of "death to America" by protestors when he returned to Tehran. Then in February 2019, Rouhani condemned the US for interfering in Venezuelan politics, once again straining US-Iranian relations.

I found other news about Iran on *Democracy Now*[18], a radio show that reports on events that the mainstream media often ignores: "The death toll from Iran's brutal crackdown on anti-government protests in November (2019) was significantly higher than previously reported, with as many as 1,500 people killed during the two weeks of demonstrations. Victims included at least 400 women and more than a dozen teenagers. The orders for the crackdown came directly from Iran's Supreme Leader Ayatollah Ali Khamenei, who reportedly told a gathering of high-level officials, 'The Islamic Republic is in danger. Do whatever it takes to end it. You have my order.'"

From Radio Farda[19]: "Iranians killed protested fuel oil increases of 50 to 200 percent." Another Radio Farda[20] states that "Iran remained in the 154th place among the 162 countries in the Human Freedom Index (HFI). The index which measures personal, civil and economic freedom at a global level, covers areas such as rule of law, security and safety, size of government, property rights, religion, civil society and expression." The US ranked 15, while "Russia, Saudi Arabia and Iran ranked 114, 149 and 154. Egypt, Venezuela and Syria are among the lowest in the index, ranking 157, 161 and 162, respectively."

Robin Wright, who has written about the Middle East for decades, in a *New Yorker* article[21] remarks that after the Iranian Revolution: "the theocracy called on women to breed a new Islamic generation. It lowered the marriage age to nine for girls and fourteen for boys; it legalized polygamy and raised the price of birth control." Family size grew, and because Tehran, a center of economic opportunity and education, quickly became over-populated, the city could no longer house all of its people. The government reconsidered its policies, and instituted family planning and built housing, "ghostly concrete towers on barren land far from the capital." There is a photo of this: the towers, white and sterile, blend in with the surrounding desert. There is no sign of life. Comparing this scenario with photos from Amol, will give you a sense of Iran being a country of contrasts.

On January 3, 2020, the US assassinated Qasem Suleimani, a top Iranian official. The world condemned this assassination by the US.[22] We all waited anxiously, wondering what Iran's response would be. Iran retaliated by launching 22 rockets at two US bases in Iraq in such a way that the US experienced no casualties. Iran even warned the US it was launching the rockets. Iran could have used the Suleimani assassination as cause for greater retribution, but chose not to.

The seminal event that those of a certain age will not forget was the Iranian Hostage Crisis: Iranian students entered the American Embassy in Tehran on November 4, 1979. (This incident is described in more detail in the following section). Fifty-two Americans were held hostage for 444 days, and treated with varying degrees of civility. How did this happen? What were relations like between Iran and the US? How did the situation deteriorate so rapidly? Before 1977, the US and Iran were allies, although at times, uneasy allies.

I rarely talked with Nasrin about Iran. It was a dangerous subject, and I certainly never mentioned the word Iran over the phone or in an e-mail, in fact any political comment was made in person, and if I happened to slip up, e-mails or texts were left unanswered. I knew that Nasrin went back to Iran to visit family, and now, after knowing what I know, and it's still very little, I think she was very courageous to visit a country whose government is so unpredictable, although many would ascertain that our government too, has become unpredictable.

The 1979 Hostage Crisis

I was 23 years-old in November 1979, living in Houston, Texas, when Iranian students entered the American Embassy in Tehran and took 52 American hostages. The hostage crisis was a huge event; I don't recall any other event that so publicly challenged the power of the US and cast doubt on our invincible image. We were intrigued and confused: how had this happened? Why were we so unprepared? How had we become so vulnerable? It's been over 40 years, and I am ashamed to admit that I did not make much effort to question the American narrative until now. I never even thought to ask Nasrin about that time in her life. I did find a video from ABC news online[23] which is an accurate account of what I remember: an American flag going up in flames, a blindfolded hostage brought out, his hands behind his back, fists raised in the air, and angry demonstrators chanting "Yankee go home!" The newscast failed to explain why the US was in Iran and what we were doing there.

Back then good Americans were encouraged to dislike and fear Iranians because they were the enemy – just as we were encouraged to dislike and fear the Russians during the Cold War. In searching for books on the Hostage Crisis I found David Farber's *Taken Hostage, The Iran Hostage Crisis and America's First Encounter with Radical Islam* (2005)[24]. This section is based, except where noted, on Farber's book, which is scholarly and solidly foot-noted.

For many years, Iran had been the pawn in the Middle East game played by Great Britain and Russia, both of which envied Iran's strategic location and desired its oil, discovered in 1909. To protect itself from Great Britain and Russia, Iran sided with the Nazis in the 1930's. Years later, to prevent the Nazis from arrogating the fields, Russia and Great Britain re-entered Iran, causing Iran, understandably, great distress. Iran's ruler, Reza Pahlavi, father to Reza Muhammad Pahlavi (the Shah who took power in 1953, the Shah of the 1979 Hostage Crisis), wrote to Roosevelt in 1941 asking for support. Although Roosevelt respected Iran's sovereignty, he declined, citing that all US efforts would be allocated to fighting WW II. However, a few years later, in December, 1943, when Roosevelt, Churchill and Stalin met in Tehran to discuss post-War issues, Roosevelt advocated for Iran's sovereignty, and persuaded the Allies to pledge to leave Iran within six months after the War's end. Because of this, Iran imagined the US was its protector. We were, for a period of time.

After the War (1946), Russia did not immediately leave northern Iran. With pressure from the US, Russia eventually left, but because the Iranian government was unstable and future Russian invasions seemed probable, the US began supplying military aid – initially not much – and economic aid – to Iran. The Cold War was gearing up, and there were many countries that the US designated as susceptible to communism. Soon, however, the US gleaned that the feared communist takeover in Iran was more likely to come from "internal revolutionary movements" rather than Russia. Iran, despite its vast oil fields, in the early 1950s, was "a poor nation filled with angry, sometimes desperate people."

It soon became apparent to Iranians that the British, who had created the Anglo-Iranian Oil Company (AIOC), were taking most of the company's profits. Aware that Saudi Arabia, Kuwait and Venezuela had negotiated 50-50 oil profit splits with foreign countries, Iran requested more equal profit-sharing. Meanwhile Britain, seething over the seizure and forthcoming nationalization of AIOC [note: the US did support Iran's request for the 50-50 split], boycotted Iranian oil, and US oil companies joined the boycott. Talks with Iran's "slippery" Mossadegh, Iran's prime minister, continued, but resolved nothing about foreign contracts or resource allocation. According to the recent documentary *Coup 53*[25], Iran's share of profits from its own oil fields was only 16 percent.

Meanwhile the British developed a secret plan to depose Mossadegh, citing his communist sympathies and unwillingness to work with Western corporations. Actually, "The West" did not sanction Mossadegh's socialist outlook.[26] Eisenhower, president in 1953, a "hardnosed" anti-communist, supported a skyrocketing military budget and the CIA's covert actions. At this time Iran's previous ruler, Reza Pahlavi, was in exile, although his young son, Reza Muhammad Pahlavi (the Shah) still lived in the royal palace. As the plot to overthrow Mossadegh was being formulated, the Shah was visited by the CIA, and although "quite nervous", agreed to become Iran's new leader.

As the overthrow proceeded in August 1953, Radio Tehran warned Iranians of the overthrow and began the virulent anti-American rhetoric that exists to this day. I'm sure many Americans would react similarly should a foreign entity attempt to topple our government. The Shah fled with his wife to Italy. (They actually discussed living in the US on a farm.) Meanwhile US-financed mobs protested in Tehran along with other groups supposedly "weary" of Mossadegh's chaotic rule.

Coup 53 describes this tumultuous period in Iran's history. The expat Britons who worked at the oil fields lived in isolation in "classic colonial enclaves". They enjoyed a cushy lifestyle and seemed to be quite dismissive of Iranians, most of whom were poor. Mossadegh, Prime Minister since 1951, was Iran's first democratically-elected Prime Minister. According to Wikipedia[27] Mossadegh was "an author, administrator, lawyer and prominent parliamentarian, and his administration introduced a range of social and political measures such as social security, land reforms and higher taxes including the introduction of taxation of the rent on land." He was well-educated, and the "first Iranian to receive a PhD in Law from a European university." He appeared in 1952 on the cover of Time magazine as the *Man of the Year*. Interestingly, the documentary mentioned that the US-Great Britain coup cost the US only $60,000. Because it went so smoothly, and involved little/no loss of life, the US became emboldened and began to meddle in the affairs of other resource-rich countries, particularly those in Central America. Guatemala in 1954, for example. It became clear to many countries that US policy which previously favored establishment of democracy, now favored acquisition of resources.

Iran eventually tried Mossadegh for treason, and put him under house arrest for the remainder of his life. He was denied communication with colleagues and friends and was not permitted to travel. However, with help from a family member, he escaped once to Tehran for a day and he marveled at how the world had changed. He died at his home, the prison imposed on him, from heartbreak.

In August 1953, the Shah returned from Italy and became the Shah of Iran. Britain, the US, and Shah negotiated the 50-50 profit split for AIOC. While AIOC was nationalized, American oil companies were given "significant advantages" in this deal. During the next eight years, the Eisenhower Administration gave over a billion dollars in economic and military aid to Iran. The number of American advisors in Iran jumped from 26 in 1952 to 207 in 1956. In 1957 the Shah formed his own "CIA": the notorious and brutal SAVAK. According to Farber: "SAVAK would become internationally infamous for the brutality, cruelty, and macabre creativity of its torturers." Meanwhile, the US believed that its activities "stabilized" Iran.

In 1960, The Shah of Iran appeared on the cover of *Time* magazine, as the *Man of the Year*. Still, the perception that the Shah was beholden to the Americans alienated the Shah from many Iranians. The American government *was* giving the Shah military aid. There were many factions in Iran fighting for power; one group, the Islamic clergy, whose power base was gaining support, opposed modernization policies, their position being that the Koran was sacred, that it formed the basis for all educational endeavors and legal rulings.

Ayatollah Khomeini, leader of Islamic Fundamentalists, communicated his anti-American and anti-modernization opinions as early as 1964: "Let the American president know that in the eyes of the Iranian people he is the most repulsive member of the human race. Let the American government know that its name has been ruined and disgraced in Iran" (Farber, 2005). Khomeini would be jailed, exiled, then later come to full power in Iran in November 1979.

Although many lauded the Shah's modernization and educational efforts, it was clear that the enormous revenue from Iran's oil wells never reached the average citizen. As the Shah grew increasingly wealthy, the government and SAVAK grew increasingly corrupt. In 1971, the Shah spent 17 to 22 million dollars on a party that celebrated Iran and his reign[28], a fact not lost on his opposition. Then from 1973 to 1975, Iran experienced hyper-economic growth due to expanded oil revenue, but most Iranians never benefited from this windfall. Rather than sharing the wealth, the Shah and his family instituted policies that maintained the status quo. Because the US deposed Mossadegh and installed the Shah, opponents asserted the US kept the Shah in power (to an extent this was true) and supported the Shah's brutal policies. President Carter, elected in 1977, and other American advisors, pressured the Shah for reforms that would give citizens additional freedom. The US, however, obtained its on-the-ground information from SAVAK, certainly not an unbiased information source.

Meanwhile the US, intent on "fighting communism" and securing the Persian oil fields, relied quite heavily on its US-Iranian alliance. After Carter was elected, debates about selling weapons to Iran increased: some in the Administration wanted to reduce arms sales, and to support only countries that gave its citizens human rights. In 1978, the Shah mildly acquiesced to US demands by giving some rights to women. This of course angered the religious conservatives. Riots and chaos ensued, and from a distance, while exiled in Iraq, Khomeini accrued followers. According to Khomeini, America was a hypocrite, a country that apparently championed freedom and human rights yet supported the Shah's "murderous regime" and its secret police, SAVAK. Khomeini's rhetoric weakened the Shah and further demonized the US. Most Americans had little interest in Iran, but the Iranians' predominant view of the US was "master string puller", and bully.

The US failed to understand the Shah's various opponents, each with their own agenda and goals, and failed to understand the dynamics that fueled the revolution. Then a theater fire in August, 1978, which killed almost 400 people, further united opposition groups. Meanwhile, the Shah lived a fantasy life in his palace, and actually did not imagine himself as an enemy of the Iranian people, nor did he believe his government to be repressive. American advisors continued to implore him to give Iranians more rights.

By late 1978, Iran was in a state of chaos. SAVAK reported to the CIA that everything was fine, that Iran "is not in a revolutionary or even pre-revolutionary situation" (Farber 2005). By November 1978, the Shah, recently diagnosed with cancer, apologized to Iranians for "past mistakes, unlawful actions, oppression and corruption." He asked the religious leaders to observe peace and order. His apology came mighty late.

In Washington, confusion reigned as the Administration vacillated between supporting and condemning the Shah. Some in Washington understood the draw and power of Khomeini (who was then 76) and suggested reaching out to him, an idea that was rejected.

On January 6, 1979, the Shah fled Iran. On February 1, 1979, Ayatollah Khomeini returned from exile in Paris to Tehran. Once in Iran, he united the pro-democracy, pro-Soviet, and Islamic Fundamentalist factions with his anti-Shah rhetoric. He promised justice and morality. He emphatically demonized the US and its avowed secularism. US intelligence continued to ignore the Islamic Revolutionaries; it failed to understand the peoples' economic grievances and was insensitive to Iran's culture and religion. Yet the US was unwilling to relinquish Iran's oil fields. US intelligence was unwilling to abandon its Russian listening post. American weapons manufacturers and US banks had billions of dollars invested in Iran.

On February 14, 1979, armed Iranians took over the American Embassy. The incident was over in an hour, yet the Administration began to reconsider its tenuous bond with Iran. Then in the summer of 1979, oil prices spiked. A war between the Khomeini run-government and Kurds in northern Iran broke out, and suddenly, Iran was ready to negotiate with the US. Khomeini needed American military parts.

Meanwhile the Shah was being treated for cancer and requested treatment in the US, the best treatment venue at the time. Khomeini wanted the Shah extradited to Iran to stand trial. Because Rockefeller's Chase Manhattan bank had loaned billions of dollars to Iran, Rockefeller lobbied the Administration to allow the Shah US entry. In October, despite clearly-stated reservations from knowledgeable advisors about an impending disaster if the Shah were allowed entry, Carter conceded, citing the Shah's need for cancer treatment and calling his entry a humanitarian act. Around that time, in October, an Iranian negotiator, Ibrahim Yazdi, had come to New York City requesting the Shah's money, and the Shah's extradition.

There was another variable. In the 1960s and 70s young people everywhere, including Iran, were looking for answers to life's soul-deadening consumeristic existence. Many flocked to religion and/or cult-like communities for answers. In Iran, these young people represented Iran's first educated generation, its new middle class, and as they questioned secularism, some found answers in traditional Islam, which experienced a resurgence of interest.

On November 2, a small group of students from Iran's four major Tehran universities asserted that if the US wasn't challenged, that if they did not act rapidly, that if they showed weakness, "then a superpower like the US will be able to meddle in the internal affairs of any nation in the world". They planned a peaceful takeover of the embassy, without weapons, and with enough food for three days.

The day the students took over the American Embassy in Tehran, November 4th, at 10 am, there were 30,000 students demonstrating in Tehran. At first, approximately 150 students entered the embassy; this number grew to 3,000. One embassy official reported that most of the students were women. One carried a sign that said, "Don't be afraid. We just want to set in." (Farber, 2005; This is in reference to the American *sit ins*.) Some Americans, however, were blindfolded and marched outside, imagining they were about to be executed. A total of 63 Americans were captured, and nine initially escaped; over the next few weeks eleven hostages – women and those with health problems – were released. The students, who believed they had Khomeini's blessing for the takeover (they did not, but Khomeini approved of the takeover after the fact), released a statement (Farber 2005):

"The Islamic Revolution of Iran represents a new achievement in the ongoing struggle between the people and the oppressive superpowers. We Muslim students, followers of Ayatollah Khomeini, have occupied the espionage embassy of America in protest against the ploys of imperialism and the Zionists. We announce our protest to the world, a protest against America for granting asylum and for employing the criminal Shah. And finally, for its undermining and destructive role in the face of the struggle of the peoples for freedom from the chains of imperialism."

The students rifled through the embassy's files, but never found proof of the CIA's attempt to overthrow the Iranian government. Yazdi, the Iranian negotiator that Carter's Administration had been working with, resigned. Khomeini declared the US to be "Satan". Russia joined in with its own pronouncements. Carter refused to give Iran the Shah, who would eventually be exiled to Panama, and then to Egypt. The world condemned the hostage taking and the US boycotted Iranian oil, and began looking elsewhere for oil. Then the Soviets invaded Afghanistan. In Iran, clashes between the leftists and Islamic Fundamentalists ensued. On April 24, 1980, Operation Eagle Claw, the American attempt to rescue the hostages involving helicopters, failed. On July 27, the Shah died in Egypt. Then in September 1980 the Iran-Iraq war began.

During those months, the Carter Administration worked day-and-night for the hostages' return, tirelessly negotiating with Khomeini, but it was only when the hostages were no longer useful (the Shah's death in July) that their release was imminent. Khomeini successfully humiliated Carter, the leader of a great superpower, by making certain that the hostages were released within minutes after Reagan took office, giving Reagan credit for their release. Even before he took office, Reagan was involved in negotiations: Reagan had promised Khomeini military aid in the scandal known as the Iran Contra Affair.

What happened to Iranians and Iranian students who were living in the US? On April 7, 1980, Carter signed *Executive Order 12170*[29] which froze all Iranian assets. Altogether, eight Executive Orders were signed. Many Iranian students had adopted the US as their home and were reluctant to return to Iran, which for many, meant death. At this time 150,000 Iranians had American visas, 56,700 of them students. There were sanctions against the students, and harassment on many campuses. While some students chanted "Nuke Iran, maim Iranians!" other students at MIT and Harvard sent a letter to Carter protesting his "selective harassment."[30] At that time, I was studying for my Master's in Geosciences at the University of Houston, and working. I was not aware of any harassment of Iranian students, but I did not know any Iranian students. Where I worked, a seismic processing company that served the US oil companies, there was a very definite ani-Iranian undercurrent. I think many of my generation, if they reflect on that unflattering period in our history, will agree that we were all encouraged to vilify Iranians.

A woman I interviewed for this book, Sarah, emigrated to the US in August 1979 when she was in the third grade. Her family settled initially in Chicago. She said: "There was a lot of *Go home you fucking*

Iranian! by the kids and the teachers. It hurt. It was really, really awful, and bad."

Part III: Reflections After a Death

Spirituality, Mourning and Grief

The idea of spirituality often came up in the interviews, along the lines of: *I became more spiritual after her passing.* Since Nasrin's death, I too, have devoted more time to exploring my own spirituality. So I started asking people for their thoughts, and tried to get an understanding of what they meant by spirituality.

Yasamin: "Spirituality is unique to each individual, it's important to them, and however or whatever gives them comfort in this life. But I think it certainly makes you, or forces you, as you lose these precious people in your life to think: 'Am I doing the best I possibly can with the time I have on this planet with the people most important to me?' Have I become more spiritual? I am not sure it's impacted me in that way. Do I feel there are things in this life that are out of my control that need a higher power? Absolutely."

Alice: "Not so much in a religious way, because I did not grow up with any particular religion, but I was interested in Eastern religions, meditation, Buddhist practices and yoga. Nasrin was interested in that. A few times I sent her chants. I don't know what her religious background was, I think she was more interested in spirituality—meditation. Especially in the last weeks when I visited her at her house and she was really frail. She liked talking about those kinds of things. I liked being peaceful around her, and she really appreciated it."

Ben: "[Spirituality] contributes to a view, I think of the world as a place in Western culture, a shining sort of idea, because people are afraid of it (death)."

Carole: "When she was sick, we talked about it (spirituality). When she went to Iran the last two times, she visited a spiritual."

Virginia: "I have always been very spiritual; it hasn't changed that. . . Nasrin was leaning more toward spirituality, not that she wasn't spiritual before, but we talked more about that in her last years."

April: "I'm pretty spiritual by nature, not necessarily in any one religion. It's an interesting question because there's aspects of it that I don't like. I definitely have more questions after her passing. Zahara and I both talked about how Nasrin had a lot of positive experiences that were otherworldly, indicating she was going to be okay. I think for me, angelic signs and those Oliver (Nasrin's grandson) signs (in dreams) are important."

Julia: "I can completely appreciate that (spirituality) especially if you're spiritual as a child, but this has never been a part of my life. Part of that is having grown up in Sweden, which is an atheist country."

Adam: "I was bought up atheist, but I think that there's something more out there. That seems strange that we'd have all of these conscious minds and thought, and that they just go away. I'm hopeful that there's something more to it."

I started paying more attention to what I read and heard on podcasts, and my definition of spirituality increasingly expanded: it need not invoke a god or higher being. Religion is not the same as spirituality, although the two are close cousins and often overlap. Religions use historical figures and stories that tend to (but not always) set people apart and close doors; spirituality's mission seems to be to open the doors, and invite all kinds of people in. Most of the following viewpoints on spirituality are from the podcast *On Being*, whose mission is to explore spirituality and life's meaning.

In one episode Joe Henry[1] equates his spiritual awakening with a musical awakening and gives resonance to the idea of mystery: "We're really called not to dispel mystery, but to abide it, to engage it. And that doesn't necessarily mean making sense of it. It's just understanding that there's a big part of this that is inherently and beautifully and romantically mysterious; the light that creates the shadow is absolutely, in so many ways, unknowable to us."

John Rowson[2] connects human spirituality with climate change: "human behavior is driven by a certain economic model. Now in that context, for the average individual trying to make sense of human existence and spiritual life, the connection isn't obviously clear. It's not obvious from our behavior that we accept this (climate change) as a real problem. And I think that is ultimately spiritual; most religious traditions confront the question of death. It's central to the fact that you're a mortal human being that you have to consider how you're going to live with the one precious life that you have."

Reverend Angel Kyodo Williams[3] says "There is so much momentum to every aspect of what drives us, what moves us, what has us hurtling through space, including all of our thoughts, and even our own sense of our emotions and how we interpret any given feeling."

An acoustic ecologist, Gordon Hempton[4], describes himself as being spiritual, but not religious, and going to church outdoors and listening to nature. "I thought that listening meant focusing my attention on what was important even before I heard it, and screening out everything that was unimportant even before I heard it."

"We are not at the pinnacle of human knowledge," Katy Payne[5], an acoustic biologist, says. That sentence stopped me cold. Visiting a zoo once and hanging nearby the elephants' compound, she felt a throbbing in her ear: elephant sounds not within our acoustic range. (She identified 70 different types of calls that elephants make.) As children, she says, we might have been aware of the sounds, but as adults, we've stopped paying attention.

It would be dishonest of me not to admit skepticism when some interviewees invoked Nasrin's presence after her passing, and maybe this battle (spirituality/god vs science) underscores my ignorance and lack of an open mind. Oliver Sacks[6], writer and neurobiologist, said of near-death and out-of-body experiences (which one interviewee commented on): "There's a sense of a last look, a (greatly accelerated) farewell to things earthly, the places and people and events of one's life and a sense of ecstasy of joy as one soars towards one's destination – an archetypal symbolism of death and transfiguration. Experiences like this are not easily dismissed by those who have been through them, and they may sometimes lead to a conversion or metanoia, a change of mind, that alters the direction and orientation of a life. Near-death experiences must also have a neurological basis of their own, one which profoundly alters consciousness itself."

Do God and Science necessarily cancel one another out? As someone who has worked in the field of science for most of my life, this has always been an unresolved question.

George Coyne[7], a Jesuit and astronomer says, that "to drag God in when we find that our science is inadequate to understanding certain events [that's] God as a god of explanation, a god of the gaps. Newton did it, you know? And every time we do it, we're diminishing God and we're diminishing science. He made a universe that I know as a scientist has a dynamism to it. It has a future that's not completely determined. We know that as scientists. Human life is so rich with life and death, with suffering, with music, and art and love and hatred. To limit our human experience to our scientific knowledge is really to impoverish all of us."

Clearly, although spirituality is a common concept, its definition is not universal, in fact its meaning varies, and sometimes widely. People define the term and abide by it in their own way.

As I interviewed people, I also began asking them how they mourned, because it did not occur to me, consciously, that people grieved differently. According to Kubler-Ross' *On Death and Dying*,[8] the bible of death back in the 1970s, the five stages of grief that people normally experience are denial, anger, bargaining, depression and acceptance. So you had your five stages and that was it.

Is that really how people mourn? What things do people do when they mourn?

"Initially, driving home after I heard, I cried," Julia said. "After the initial shock we just felt upset. I'm desensitized, I see a lot of death, and I'm a pragmatist. I think: I'm going to let this remind me of how precious life is and not take life for granted. I get upset when I think about what my mother lost because she lost someone who was very close to her."

"I look at photographs," Carole said. "People that have passed on appear in my dreams. Nasrin, but I can't give you specifics. I do pray for people that have passed as well. So I am a lapsed Catholic, it's through prayer but yes, the religion."

"It's not always with people," April said. "One thing that helps me is being in the space that I shared with that person. Her house – being in that space and remembering all of it, the good and the bad, then just keeping memories and letting them go simultaneously. It's been a longer process than I anticipated. Zahara and I both talked about how Nasrin had a lot of positive experiences that were otherworldly, indicating she was going to be okay."

"By feeling her presence and remembering her," Hannah said. "The last time I went to Iliad to Zahara's house, the first time since Nasrin passed away, I felt special being in that space. I definitely felt her presence. I remember the last time I saw Nasrin. It was in Boston, I spent a couple of days at Zahara's and Adam's, just hanging out with them. Nasrin looked really good. We had some food, and she made us tea. She was really happy to be with her grandson and feeling good. I think about that day a lot. That's how I want to remember Nasrin."

"We see reminders of her every day," Adam said. "Zahara and Oliver talk about her every day. Mourning is how you think about situations. Sometimes, everything reminds you of her."

"I'm not really sure how I mourn," Ben said, "I learned from school that there's no real set stage of mourning, despite some psychologists saying there are, it's very different for each person. It's further different for each person who has died. There's different relationships in each death, and for each person to think about another person. I cried a few times. I try to flock to the people who are still alive and offer support to them. Because I can't in any way justify some sort of connection with me to god, it's very abstract, but people get to know a sense of god, depending on how much they meditate."

"I'm not one who cries much," Carolyn said. "I care deeply and I get melancholic. One forgets that they're ageing, I'm ageing, it could happen to me, to anyone I love. The fear – I try not to go with that because whatever our assignment is, the final assignment is to leave here. But that doesn't make it any less sad when someone you loved has fulfilled their assignment. It doesn't seem real. I try not to think of her as being erased from existence. She still exists for me and I know her soul is there. How do I mourn? Not with complete annihilation: I mourn because I can't talk to her, I can't pick up the phone and that makes me sad and I miss her."

"Nasrin's grave is close to my house and I walk nearly every day," Sorayya said, "so I do visit her grave sometimes. Visiting is paying respect and giving. At her grave I say a Muslim prayer, a Quranic verse that you repeat three times when you go to someone's grave. Every time I go, I feel the earth has swallowed her up more. The grass is growing over it and there's less and less an imprint. Somehow she still feels alive, not just in Zahara but in daily events. Sometimes when I wake up in the morning and see the sun rising I think if Nasrin could see the colors she would be astonished. When I stand there (at the grave) I feel a closeness to Nasrin, I almost hear her laughing. It's important to respect her memory; it's not only respecting the dead but also a way of confronting what's going to happen to all of us, and it's important for us to do that. We mourn by absorbing loss, you have more respect for the beauty and joy and love in life. So remembering Nasrin on a beautiful day when I go to Stewart Park is also a way of mourning. It's a more hopeful way."

"Sadness, crying and an intense sense of loneliness," Yasamin said. Her husband passed away a few months after Nasrin. "Just trying to find resources, to understand, trying to figure out how not to be alone. I'm going through it, but I don't know what I'm going through, the feelings of it, the mechanics of it, reading and trying to find solace and being with people that I love."

"I think it's so important to have some kind of memorial," Alice said. "There are people who don't do that because they feel it's egocentric, or something like that. Nasrin's was just beautiful. It was such a key piece. My friend whose husband died this summer, she is amazing, she's keeping it conscious, and reaching out to her friends and she's talking about it. That's a really important thing to do, as painful as it is. It gets even more painful if you don't."

"For me, the best thing was to visit Zahara and talk," Virginia said. "Going to Boston and spending time with her was something that brought me comfort. I felt that I was doing something good for Zahara and for Nasrin. Here people talk a lot about what they do for grieving. I don't recollect that as being part of a conversation when I grew up, even though there were several deaths in my family. When a person dies, you are sad, and you keep going. [Virginia is Argentinian.] You pray or you don't pray, you mourn in different way, but we don't talk about grieving. My husband has the same recollection from India. Seeing it from an anthropological perspective, I think it's a cultural thing."

"Because of my MS," Sue said, "I've had it over 40 years and I've been doing pretty good with it, trying not to get stressed out, so I haven't been very good at mourning."

"I feel the pain of her loss as a huge hole in my heart," Susan said. "I miss her every day. For the first nine days I went to the cemetery every day. I needed to help her adjust to her new state. I verbally introduced her to her new 'neighbors.' It seemed right, knowing how focused on others Nasrin was. But I have to het her go. I don't want to interfere with the peace I hope she's found. She's released from her earthy cares! She's escaped the clutches of cancer and I hope she's safe in her dad's arms now. I don't go daily anymore. Maybe every two days, sometimes two nights in a row. It's comforting to have a place to feel close to her. Sometimes I bring flowers. And I had this crazy thought of digging her up. We all do a little bit (caring for the grave, planting flowers) and that is comforting. Three groups of petunias become balm for the pain because someone else showed up and remembered her too."

"It's hard," Zahara said. "I'm trying to allow myself to feel what I'm feeling. Instead of fighting some of these emotions, intense emotions, just allowing yourself to have them. I focus on more of the good memories of her because there were a lot of horrible ones at the end. The good ones help. I believe that spirits live on after death. I talk to her and maybe that sounds like a crazy person, but it helps. It makes me feel like I'm still close to her."

In a short TED talk Nora McInerny[9] says *We don't move on from grief, we move forward with it.* People tend to forget that "Grief doesn't happen in a vacuum, it happens alongside of and mixed in with all these other emotions."

George Bonanno[10] along with his colleagues, interviewed hundreds of grief-stricken individuals to define *what grief was really like.* Bonanno's conclusions did not always agree with Kubler-Ross's or Freud's; Freud said you have to *do the hard work of grief,* which meant resurrecting memories. Bonanno says: "Memories of people are clusters of snakelike neurons, arranged in branching pathways throughout the brain." The *hard work of grief* can in fact, be detrimental, especially for those forced to go to grief counseling; grief counseling can be an irritation rather than a help. As for Kubler-Ross' five stages, Bonanno and colleagues found that some go through them, some don't.

Everyone grieves differently and works through grief in her own way.

"Bereavement," Bonanno says, "is a human experience. It is something we are wired for, and it is certainly not meant to overwhelm us." He contends that most people are resilient. He added that "even the most resistant /resilient seemed to hold onto at least a bit of wistful sadness. But we are able to keep living out our lives and loving those still present around us. [Most] bereaved people are able to have genuinely pleasurable experiences, to laugh or indulge in moments of joy, even in the earliest days and weeks of loss. Not only are positive experiences common, but they also tend to have an affirmative impact on other people and may actually help the bereaved recover more quickly after the loss. In general, sadness helps us focus and promotes more effective reflection."

Andy Pruddicombe narrator of the *Headspace Grieving Course*[11] (which I listened to several times) says the idea is to "create a space where the body and mind can come to a place of greater ease." The initial numbness, he says, is a difficult feeling to sit with because of its unfamiliarity. "We want a more intense emotion to assure ourselves we are feeling." He suggests we "step out long enough to momentarily reconnect with that feeling of that relationship. Acknowledge the feeling, step out, come back to the breath."

In late August 2019 I was walking around a landscape with a recent widow, taking photos and notes, deciding where we would weed and prune, where we would mulch. My company was prepping her landscape for her husband's memorial service. "I would like to have a job like yours," she said, and she raised her gaze to her empty house. For me, digging my hands into soil, feeling and smelling the earth, pulling weeds, planting wildflower seeds, seeing bees and other insects congregating is a way to grieve: it's how I reconnect with something solid. The solidity centers me and it creates an image in my mind that I can take with me everywhere. Feel, step out, come back to the breath. I hoped that the widow had a similar centering activity.

"We are never finished with grief," V.S. Naipaul[12] says in his *Grief, A writer reckons with loss*. "It is part of the fabric of living. It is always waiting to happen. Love makes memories and life precious; the grief that comes to us is proportionate to that love and is inescapable. We can never tell beforehand for whom we will feel grief." He mentions his younger brother's death and his inability to eat. "It made my grief concrete, and it lasted all week." At the crematorium as an attendant invited V.S. to place his hand on the coffin, he says: "The rites of death were completely new to me; this was the comfort that many before me had instinctively sought. It didn't work for me." He adds: "My sorrow lasted for two years. For two years I mentally dated everything, even the purchase of a book, by its distance from Shiva's death."

Katy Payne[13] describes an elephant community's reaction to a calf's death where over 100 elephants visited the dead calf to "express concern." Most of the elephants were not related biologically to the dead calf. One quarter of the mourning elephants tried to lift the dead calf's body. One adolescent tried 57 times.

Anna and I are in Zagreb. It's a Sunday in February and the one museum she wants to visit, *The Museum of Broken Relationships*, is open. It sounds gimmicky but once inside, as I walk among the displays and read the descriptions of how much a sock puppet meant to a lover, what a simple stone said about a person who had been deeply loved, I change my mind. There was an audio tape that a Japanese mother had made of her son and his father when the son was a baby. Her hope, and it came to pass, was that the son would find the tape (after his father died) and have this remembrance. There was *The Toaster Vindicated: I'm gone, no more toast*. Because the museum gives grief a concrete solidity, it makes grief more familiar, accessible, easier to share and less complicated. There were hand-written notes, drawings, stones (male and female), *The New Yorker* cover of two female brides, a star chart, a bike, shoes, boots, two bras (a woman losing her breasts), the end of the affair with *Chef Boyardee Pizza* (gluten intolerance), a religious figure, a prosthetic leg, an ugly orange stand-up light, a Godzilla loaded with gaudy necklaces. A perfect white wedding dress stands alone, waiting for a woman to inhabit the gown. The note beside it says that a week before the wedding, the bride-to-be's fiancé was killed in a terrorist attack. You can't help feeling the woman's sadness.

My favorite is a VHS tape of a father's second marriage to a horrible co-worker. After the marriage, the co-worker immediately quit her job, spent the father's money, then refused to pay for his hospice care as he lay dying. The father's son and daughter, finding the wedding tape of the father's marriage, proceeded to destroy it: they ran over it, attacked it with a screwdriver, chopped it with an ax, burnt it, then proclaimed: "It was the best therapy."[14] I could see myself doing the exact same thing.

The exhibits were quirky and funny, sad and melancholic. During that afternoon of sighs and nods of acknowledgement, it was hard not to feel bewitched by these odd contributions to humanity. Some images have a power that resonates within you and lodges in your mind.

What else does grief propel us to do? How do we find release? In the early 1980s I ran compulsively every day for over a year, at noon in Houston, on concrete roads, no shade. I was thin, amenorrheic and miserable. My company was going through a takeover, so all work essentially stopped. I had no friends, my marriage was in disarray, and the day I quit my job, I stopped running. I no longer felt the need to run. Just like that: the line between then and now as sharp as the full moon's image on a cloudless cold night.

A close friend of mine, a very progressive single-mom whose only child went to college, cried and cried when he left. She decided to attend Catholic Mass. She did nearly every day for three months then someone vandalized her bike which she had parked outside the church. *Enough,* she said, *the trance has been broken.*

"Time. It allows emotions to dissipate and helps us regain perspective," ODLpodcast[15].

Death

Each death, as it brings us closer to our own death, gives us a nudge: Listen to yourself, know where you stand in the larger Universe.

Commenting on Nasrin's death, Marie said: "It really hammered home in a very palpable way the preciousness of life and the temporary nature of existence."

"With her particularly, it opened my mind to the importance of life," Julia said.

Noni: "Preparing for my own death certainly. And you'd want to discuss this with your kids."

"I woke up the next morning," Zhila said, "and thought, *How am I going to handle this?* We saw burial places and the service place and we did everything in one day. It was an amazing experience for me, I had never been with someone at the passing moment. Nasrin had pain, but that was what she wanted, and I admire Zahara. Noni helped with all of the arrangements: she did all of the research. All the energy forces helped us."

Sue: "I don't think about that [my own death] now that I have had this little stroke. I am 66 and my parents both died at 69. [Still] It's very hard not to be able to pick up the phone and talk to her and see how things are going with Zahara and Oliver. We used to talk about everything."

Sorayya: "It adds to the register of grief. It makes me think so much about Zahara because I feel such a loss when my mother died, and I was not as close to my mother as Nasrin and Zahara were, but I feel such emptiness and it's difficult to come to terms with it."

"It makes life more precious," Alice said. "When someone has touched you as Nasrin did, I feel emotion rising when I think about her.

A piece of her is ingrained. You remember deeply her eyes, her kindness, her courage. Incredible sweetness and grace. Hopefully some of this rubbed off on me."

"It makes you think about your relationship with your own mother," Hannah said, "how you would feel if your own mother passed away."

"It definitely reminds you that you won't want to waste your life," Adam said, "because you really only have the present moment. We're always planning for the future – too much – and forget to live in the present moment. Nasrin reminds you to make the most of whatever you do have."

"It makes me more aware of my mortality," Carolyn said, "and I had better savor my moments because you never know. It's heartbreaking, but it does make me want to be more grateful for my life."

"There's no doubt when someone dies who is close to me it makes me think about mortality," Ben said. "We're all mortal, we're all animals. We're part of the wild. We die just as other beings do. And I'm just a bit ashamed that I feel in some ways positive, that I'm able to keep going, whether or not that's a testament or an insult to those who died."

"I have lost too many friends to cancer," Carole said. "I think about her often, in a happy way. I know it's making April and me talk more. When someone close to you dies, your death becomes more real. For me, it's the sadness of Zahara and the grandkids, not so much for me."

"It's hard," April said. "It affected me more than I could have predicted. This one's much harder because she was relatively young, she's probably the person I've known the longest who has passed. She was pretty much a parent: I called her Mom and she called me Daughter. She was just such a rock. The life experiences that she's missing are really hard for me, like Zahara being pregnant, meeting her second grandchild, or meeting Hannah's."

"My priorities in life are completely different," Zahara said. "I used to work a stressful job, work my way up the ladder and make a lot of money. None of that matters anymore. I want to be happy and healthy and be a really good Mom to my children. It all blends together. I've become a more compassionate person. With others going through tough times I used to feel awkward reaching out, now I want to be there for people in any way I can."

"I think about death differently, and a lot," Susan said. "I wish Nasrin had taken the morphine sooner, yet being the person she was, who honored her body and ate healthfully and avoided medications, it made sense that she waited two weeks before dying to take the morphine."

Peter Schjeldahl[16] after receiving a diagnosis of cancer: "I had a moment, while anticipating my diagnosis, of feeling special. But what's as commonplace as dying? Everybody does it." He ends his essay with: "Oddly, or not, I find myself thinking about death less than I used to. Why me? Why not me? In point of fact, me dying is my turn to survey life from its far – now near – shore. God creeps in. Human minds are the universe's only instruments for reflecting on itself. If God is a human invention, good for us! We had to come up with something. Take death for a walk in your minds, folks. Either you'll be glad you did or, keeling over suddenly, you won't be out anything."

There's a 1950's episode of *The Twilight Zone* [17], one of the series' first episodes, where Death visits the pitchman: a kind salesman who befriends the neighborhood children. The pitchman is in his 60s, and doesn't want to die. Suddenly you hear a car's brakes screeching. *I have to take someone*, Death says. Unable to bear the death of a young child, the pitchman gives the pitch of his life and convinces Death to take him instead.

In late September, Anna and I drive to Nasrin's grave. There is no headstone. There are some mums holding their own. I notice the three ninebarks nearby that Nasrin had planted on her property, still I call Zahara verifying that we have the right grave. We plant daffodils, multicolored hyacinths, hoping that the squirrels don't dig them up. I always admired Nasrin's landscape of stone and roses, and her ninebarks. The August that Oliver turned one, Mike and I visited and became intrigued by the bee activity surrounding the ninebarks: the shrubs were not only covered with bees, but there were four or five varieties of bees. This memory reminds me again of how she left the world a better place.

***

Sorayya mentioned the register of death. As we age and our register grows, if we're sensible, we'll make time to reflect on past deaths.

The first death of anyone close to me was my cousin, Michael Murray. He was a *blue baby* who had a *hole in his heart* and was predicted to live to age 12. He surprised everyone by completing his first year of college, then dying of a heart attack while driving home from a party. He was 19. I was 15. My aunt had been building a new house and I remember walking onto the kitchen floor, which was plywood at the time, and being surprised at her hair: it seemed to have turned white overnight. That Michael appeared in dreams with three red roses in his hand was a sign to my aunt that he was okay, that he made it to Heaven. The smell of funeral flowers followed me for months, the tale of the Three Red Roses will be with me forever.

All of my grandparents have died, and most of my aunts and uncles. My time is coming.

I was in a hospital in Bismarck, North Dakota, on November 9, 1989. A TV high in one corner of the room showed Germans sledgehammering the Berlin Wall and breaking it apart wherever they could. I was the only one in that hospital wing. (I had a stillborn). I had felt invincible and entitled to a child, but this death caused a gear to slip in my brain: I had missed an important message while growing up that one's control over the world is limited. It was something I needed to be reminded of. I distinctly remember reasoning how little life the baby had, whereas I had been alive already for 33 years.

I flew to Florida in late February 2005, to be with my dad, and then two weeks later for his memorial service. I missed his death because my son, Ben was ill. (He was diagnosed five months later with lymphoma.) My dad was 77 and the cancer that he survived 12 years earlier returned. There was lots of drama and chaos: doors were removed from hinges. Signs were hung on other doors: *Home of the Wicked Witch* – in reference to my mom. There was a brutal battle over hospice care, inappropriate use of meds, and a blindingly white wedding dress and veil worn at the service by a family member who declared herself to be the *Bride of Jesus*. Death and its aftermath are never, in my experience, what one expects.

I don't know if any deaths are smooth, but it seems worthwhile to contemplate those in your register and your own death. As a person *who treads lightly upon the earth*, I have already conveyed to my children my zero-waste disposition and preference for Newfield's green cemetery. As an adherent of the cradle-to-grave philosophy, I want to continue to feed the trees and wildflowers – this time with my own organic material – but without the added poison.

There is now, in some states, a home funeral movement whose mission is to give control back to the family, and away from the funeral industry.[18] It's organized by home death-care guides who prepare the body of loved ones for home viewing. Family and friends are encouraged to visit, talk, sing, reminisce and say goodbye. Researchers found that most cultures (in a study of 57) "included death rituals in which people viewed corpses. In 90 percent of those cultures the families also had some physical contact with the bodies; such rituals suggest that they have a therapeutic value, perhaps helping the living to grieve and accept that a person has died. Given a choice, many people wanted to see a dead loved one after a traumatic death; it made the death real to them, or it allowed them to say goodbye, or they felt they owed it to the dead person." Seeing the dead body "is the hardest and most helpful part of accepting that a death is real."

In the podcast, *Call Your Girlfriend*, death acceptance activist and funeral industrial complex reformer, Caitlin Doughty,[19] says: "If I had to sum up my job in one sentence it would be dead bodies are not dangerous. It's my deepest truth that I need to express to the universe which is that we need to redeem the image of the dead body. Because I see the dead body as an incredibly useful tool for grieving, for engaging with your own mortality. So when mom dies at home, yeah there's absolutely a primal fear of just being alone with your own mother. That somehow she transmogrifies immediately upon her death into some creature that's actively decomposing and threatening you in some way and call a professional. It's an emergency. Get someone to get her out of here right now."

"It's completely safe and completely legal to just chill out with mom for a little while. I only ever hear pretty positive things about that experience, and sometimes very, very extremely positive things about how just settling into a moment with mom and seeing that she's no longer suffering, seeing that her breathing isn't labored, seeing that she's okay now. She's still. She's silent. Seeing the small changes that remind you that she is dead now. That's an important thing to take in and start your grieving process because it's not going to start and end in that room. It's going to be a long, long process. But kicking that off with I did some final things to care for my mother just like she cared for me growing up. I washed her face. I closed her mouth. I held her hand. I was present with her. I gave her that. I gave myself that."

In Iliad we have death cafes, where people can gather and talk honestly with one another about death. Susan told me about them, and I plan to attend the next one, assuming we have the required social distancing.
And to Anna, Laurie and Ben: now you know my wishes.

Friendship

This is the story of my friendship with Nasrin. It's also a meditation on the friendships that women build together. I would be walking or biking, and I would stop, pause, take a few deep breaths, listen, and think about Nasrin and other close friends.

I began my interviews with: *Tell me about yourself,* so here's my story.

When I was nine years old, I met a geologist at Yellowstone National Park who explained how rhyolite – a purple igneous rock with a smattering of quartz grains – formed. From that moment on, I was hooked: rocks can tell stories? Behind the house that I grew up in is a deep deciduous woods transected by creeks, and as a youngster, I would explore the creek beds for fossils. I also fossil-hunted along the shores of Lake Erie where my grandmother lived. Since age nine I have thought of myself as a scientist and viewed the world from the framework of The Scientific Method. Whenever I come across a rock landscape, I try to identify the rock and speculate on how the rock came into being, and where the rock fits in the world's larger geological context. For instance, the fossils in Iliad were formed and preserved in a Devonian ocean, about 400 million years ago. I can't even imagine a million years, let alone 400.

While living in Houston in the late 1970s and early 1980s, and having completed a Masters in GeoSciences, I finally had time to take some non-science courses. One course, *The City and The Flaneur,* taught by Phillip Lopate, had a homework requirement to keep a journal. I took the class to heart as I described the city from the viewpoint of a cyclist (I had no car) and a loner (I had no friends). I took more writing and literature classes, and when I moved to Madison,

Wisconsin, I convinced an engineer at the University's Engineering Department to hire me to write for the EPA. Still, the journal writing that started in the 1980s had become as much of a habit as breathing, and I have filled dozens of one-dollar notebooks with anything and everything. At first it was a requirement, but then writing became my way of making sense of the world, and making sense of who I am.

The mind is assaulted with thousands of impressions every day. According to Cornell[20] researchers we make 35,000 decisions – 227 amazingly, just on food – every day! How can a person even organize these impressions unless you give yourself time to sit back and reflect? What's important? What do you pursue? What do you throw away? Added to that, one doesn't always know in the moment the worthiness of an impression or an idea.

I grew up outside of Buffalo, New York. There was a farm up the hill where we'd buy eggs. Every spring my family planted a huge vegetable garden (we had a tractor, my father grew up on a farm), hence, the familiar feel of soil on my hands, and the exquisite pleasure of seeing a seed push its way out of the earth.

I've worked since the age of 13, as a sitter, house cleaner, fast food server, underage stadium beer seller, cafeteria worker (college). I moved to Houston two weeks after college graduation and worked in a bar, a pool hall, graduated to a radar data and seismic processor, then to a geologist at Gulf Oil. I quit Gulf Oil and taught middle school science and computer science at a Catholic middle school, St. Augustine's, in south Houston. I moved again, this time to the D.C. area, and I taught computer software and became a science consultant, then an EPA science writer while living in Madison, Wisconsin, then in Bismarck, North Dakota, and finally Shoreview, Minnesota. Anna was born in Madison, Laura in Bismarck, Ben in Shoreview. We moved to Iliad in 1996 and I became a substitute teacher, a high school science teacher, a tutor, director of a non-profit, lab worker, all until 2010 when I secured a job at a landscaping company. There I started at the bottom as a receptionist/invoicer, but after passing the Certified Nursery Landscape Professional exam, I moved up.

I became an estimator and a landscape troubleshooter.

We moved to Iliad because my husband had grown up here, and has family here. Initially we rented a house in the neighborhood known as Northeast, on Texas Lane, then a month later, we bought a house in

C. Heights. This meant that my two older children had to switch schools, which for Anna, meant three different schools in 18 months, in addition to the confusion that her parents' relationship caused. She was miserable. But the misery dissipated when Zahara, Anna's real first friend in Iliad, invited her over to the house on Hook Place.

I met Nasrin in 1997 and one of the first questions I asked Nasrin was if there were other children. *Just me and Zahara,* she said, her accent signaling she was not born in the US. Later Nasrin mentioned she was Iranian. She was the first Iranian I had ever met, and I met other Iranians because of her. My family had participated in Buffalo World Hospitality, which meant we hosted Koreans, Indians, Nigerians, Germans, and became particularly good friends with an Indian researcher who gave my brother a leftover research bat. The health department later removed the bat. (Rabies.) So having friendships with people who were not American was not so unusual. And my ex's parents, born in Budapest and Antwerp, entered the US in their teens. There was family, so to speak, who were recent immigrants.

And the more I began to learn about Nasrin, the more in awe of her I became. She mentioned she was divorced, and to divorce without family support is a very difficult undertaking. In 1997 I was poised on the precipice of my own divorce. The ideas that pass between two women that are never verbalized – those can be the most powerful ideas – and can compel one to act. By September 1998 I was divorced. I did have some family support but my divorce was still difficult. And I came to Iliad with my EPA-writing job, and although it wasn't a lucrative gig, it was a job, and I had savings. I had advantages that Nasrin never had, but like Nasrin, I had a friend who I had recently met, and who became a vital emotional support throughout the ordeal.

Nasrin bought her own house on West Hill, on Hook Place, on the blue-collar side of town where housing was not so expensive. Unwilling to change Anna's and now Laura's schools *again*, I began house-hunting on West Hill. I remember walking into my present house in March (and not knowing that this was also the road where Nasrin babysat Debbie's boys), the deciduous trees on the hills barren of leaves, and walking up the stairs. I glanced at the view over the valley to the east ridge. It was stunning. It took me five minutes to say *Yes. This house.*

When I had my first mammogram later that year at Guthrie Medical, Nasrin just happened to be my radiographer. I don't remember our conversation, but after that, we became friends. That fast. And no one else did my mammograms until Nasrin left Guthrie. There aren't many people who can say they look forward to that painful, boob-squeezing experience, but with Nasrin it was a pleasure. She was the one who walked me through the process when I needed a breast biopsy. Having an insider watching out for you during a medical procedure gives you an added layer of protection and sanity.

We were both busy with kids and jobs, and trying to keep our houses from collapsing. Both of our houses had water problems.

As with any good friend, every interaction with Nasrin was another opportunity to learn about each other and cement the bonds of friendship. Nasrin and sometimes Zahara, would come to our annual *Day After Event* – a gathering held shortly after Christmas for those of any religion or no religion. I had been brought up as a strict Catholic, but at 16, I left the Church aghast at how it treated women as second-class people. Years later the whole pedophile drama erupted.

Like Nasrin, I returned to college. I graduated from Cortland State with a Professional Teaching degree. Anna, who was 12, was in charge of the other two from after school until 9 pm, two nights-a-week. When Nasrin worked at the hospital there were times that she had no choice but to bring Zahara with her.

I remember walking into my adolescent psychology course at Cortland State, September 11, 2001, when I saw on the TV at the classroom's front, the South Tower collapsing. Like most, my first thought was: *What just happened?* Later it became: *How could anyone hate us this much?* For days I listened attentively to the radio trying to get information. I read newspapers and magazines and happened to hear Noam Chomsky on the radio program, *Democracy Now.* Chomsky's opinions did not fall in line with the country's: *We are protecting our oil.* Chomsky's stories were different, and I started paying attention to them. And I started paying closer attention to my friends from the Middle East.

I was 17 during the Arab Oil Crisis of 1973. If your license plate number ended with an odd number, you could buy gas on odd-numbered days, similarly, with an even number, you could buy gas on even-numbered days. I can't remember waiting in line for gas for more than a few minutes, but I know that some gas stations ran out of gas. I did not own a car until I graduated from college, so I wasn't directly affected by the oil crisis. I did not know much of anything about the Middle East: every history class I had ever taken was about dates and events, and lacked any real assessment of other cultures, and people: about who they were, how they lived, and what they wanted for their lives.

An incident stands out during my four years in college. I was a senior and the student manager of a cafeteria. An African American student came through the cafeteria line. This was a typical Sunday morning and most students had had a bit too much beer the previous night. The young man was being disruptive, and had been in the past, or at least I believed he had been, and as the student manager, I had to do something, so I said, "Why can't you act like a human?"

It was an arrogant and unfair statement. Years later, it occurred to me that he was a black man in a predominately white central New York liberal arts university. I had no idea what his background was, who he was, or what the altercation was about. Maybe he had been in the war. I had an acquaintance whom I never got to know well, with needle marks up and down his arms. The rumor was that he had been in the Vietnam War. Maybe this disruptive student too, had been in a war? A different kind of war?

Fast forward to the summer of 1978, and I had moved to Houston having been bequeathed the family's 1972 Pinto, which died a few days after my arrival. I lived during that first summer in an apartment without an air conditioner and worked as a pool hall attendant (never got paid), a cocktail waitress at Dome Shadows, near the Astrodome, then as a waitress at Denny's until I secured a job at Western Geophysical. There I was, one of many 20-somethings in a cafeteria-sized room counting seismic traces and inputting the data into computer programs. Raytheon CRTs had just been developed so we didn't need to use the cardboard computer cards anymore. This was in 1979. On November 4, 1979, 63 Americans had been taken hostage in Tehran at the American Embassy. At the far end of our room was a door-sized, black-and-white poster of Ayatollah Khomeini. When the seismic processors needed a break, they would take a dart and throw it at Khomeini.

At that time I did not know anyone from the Middle East and had never met anyone from that part of the world. In the neighborhood where I grew up, there were Czechoslovakians, Poles, Italians, Germans, all mostly second-generation, and some who held onto their accents and culture. My parents were not political in any sense except for one action. There were three African American families in my town, Orchard Park. One was a doctor, and he became my mom's doctor, and mine. My mom had rheumatic fever and laid in bed for a year recuperating. That was the cure back in the early 60s. When I asked her how Dr. Dunn became her doctor, she said, *He was a nice guy. And I liked him.* He also came to the house. I remember them always laughing and joking. He probably did not admonish her for her diet of Coke and potato chips. That wasn't in itself a political act, but more or less an affirmation of who my mom was. She mentioned once that the Orchard Park Country Club and Hickory Hill swim club (we joined the latter – in summer our well would dry up and showering was impossible) wouldn't give him a membership, so he built his own pool. *Take that,* my Mom seemed to say.

Those odd, apparently disconnected things that happen to you, that seem out of the norm because they are, you think about them, and years later, if you're lucky, and if you meet the right people, they can help you begin to understand what happened, and give you some understanding of who you are, and the vastness of the world, and an understanding of how much you still do not know about the world.

After 9-11, the US was all the more intent on creating the Us vs Them mentality with the Middle East, a duality that previously applied to communism. But this time, I had very close friends who were apparently "Them"; yet for me, they were "Us". In 2003, Anna and I had bus reservations to D.C. to protest the war in Afghanistan, but the flu terminated our plans.

Then in 2007, just before I had turned 51, I lost my job at Iliad High School. *We don't want to put any more time into you*, the Principal said, as if I was a plant that could be turned toward the light, then away, and therefore re-trained. I had wanted to teach since the 1980s, when I first taught at St. Augustine's in south Houston. Catholic schools do not require teaching certificates, but by the time Iliad High School *let me go*, I had completed all required New York State coursework. I had four science teaching certifications.

I told Nasrin I had lost my job. Then I went over to her house on Terrace View and she cut my hair and dyed it. She gave me clothes to wear. She gave me makeup and told me how to use it. We decided that if I looked younger, I'd have a better shot at a job. Sue was over, I don't remember why, but I vaguely remember her: I was reeling from my job loss and my predominant concern was to pool all energy and brain power and get another job. The future I had planned for was gone. This is where friends (and not just Nasrin, but other friends too) enter into your internal monologue and they say: *You can do this. Don't give up. You will find something.* After two years, and six full/part-time jobs (four jobs at one time), a landscaping company hired me. Working there gave me another topic of mutual interest with Nasrin: she always had a tidy and interesting landscape: roses, irises, ninebark, mint, and crown vetch down a hillside toward a main road into the city.

A coworker of mine who went to school for industrial design told me, *I can walk into a room and in seven seconds tell you four important things about a person.* He could deconstruct smiles, eye movements, and tone of voice. He was taught this skill, but for Nasrin, it was intuition.

To say Nasrin has been an influence on my life is an understatement. To say, as others have mentioned, that I was grateful for her presence in my life, is an understatement.

What is gratefulness? How can we practice gratitude? "There is a very simple kind of methodology to it: Stop, look, go," David Steindl-Rast[21], a Benedictine Monk, says. "So the first thing is that we have to stop, because otherwise we are not really coming into this present moment at all, and we can't even appreciate the opportunity that is given to us, because we rush by, and it rushes by. When you are in practice, a split second is enough. And if we really see what the opportunity is, we must, of course, not stop there, but we must do something with it: Go. Avail yourself of the opportunity. And if you do that, if you try practicing that at this moment, tonight, we will already be happier people, because it has an immediate feedback of joy." He adds: "There are many things for which you cannot be grateful. But in every moment, you can be grateful."

Nasrin's diagnosis in March 2016 became that wakeup call that forced me to assess my priorities, especially with respect to work. *It's necessary to have money, but some money, because there's only so much time that one has,* so my inner monologue went. *What do I need and want to do with my remaining time?* The onset of Nasrin's illness compelled me, that week, to ask my boss to work fewer hours. Two colleagues of mine at work had died recently, and they were friends, but not so close; close friends I can count on my one hand.

Then a few months later the Cancer Resource Center referred Nasrin to a free meditation at St. Luke's Church near CU's campus. Nasrin went, I did too, but my back ached from the child's chair that I sat on and I declared that once was enough. In addition, the facilitator, who recognized he had a captive audience, couldn't help but practice his preaching skills. Sorayya said, *Try a different chair. And I'm going in part, to support Nasrin.* Supporting Nasrin was a good enough argument so I went the next week, found a bigger chair, then mentally prepared myself for the preaching segment. It wasn't so bad, so I kept going.

Other acquaintances of Nasrin's came: Zhila, Zahara, Carole West's son. There were often CU students, and other community people. The preaching facilitator eventually got a job in Silicon Valley, and his co-facilitator, Sevag, another CU Ph.D. student, whose gentleness enveloped the room and softened the edges of our day, assumed leadership. For a few years, I went nearly every other week. I still attend now, 4:30 Thursday Zoom sessions, COVID-19 compelling us all to remain at home. Nasrin often mentioned that the meditation overwhelmed her with emotion, that she had gotten to that deep place. I had meditated since the 1970's, but the CU meditation reinforced my general practice. The end-of-the-week meditation with Sevag was always something I looked forward to. Nasrin and I had talked about attending the Tibetan Monk meditation on South Hill. I went once, but I don't think Nasrin ever got the chance to.

Nasrin worked at the Guthrie Clinic in Iliad for over 20 years. When she was diagnosed with cancer, Guthrie took her job away, but not immediately: they played a cat-and-mouse game with her, and Nasrin could have taken legal action, but the extra stress would have cost her in terms of health. Instead, Nasrin reinvented herself, again and again, searching for economic opportunity and survival. When Nasrin bought the house on Terrace View, she immediately remodeled the garage into a rentable apartment. Good move. She started a beauty salon – trimming eyebrows and hair – but most of the work she did for free, for friends. She started a business: *Basil and Thyme Food Catering*, and her food was a big hit but the work was grueling, especially because the chemo exhausted her. *Basil and Thyme* was accepted into the Farmer's Market but it was a gamble, and she decided not to pursue it. Nasrin returned to school, Empire State, got another degree, then studied for several months to get a Real Estate license. She turned her house into an Airbnb and was considering daycare/elder care when she moved to Boston to be with Zahara, Adam and Oliver.

Nasrin's friendships with Iliadians really starts with Sue in 1986, before Zahara was born. Sue took a risk and said yes to a couple, and in particular, the woman who barely spoke any English. I have to wonder what passed between the two of them when they met one another, because for sure, we are always signaling to other people with our body language, our eyes and with that hopeful smile. *Give me a chance.*

A good friend is able to reach your inner being and mirror back to you some of the essence of who you are. Because you care about that person, her words have the power and weight to compel you to pause, and to contemplate. A close friend reveals your virtues and your flaws; her assembled version of who you are will be different from your version, and this disconnection forces you to examine your opinions and beliefs, and as it does, it gives you perspective, it guides you when making those critical decisions that define the direction of your life. A good friend 'has your back'; she supports you in becoming the best person possible, and educates you in a myriad of ways, and fills in the gaps of ignorance that we all have, but in the kindest way possible.

A good, close friend breaks down barriers.

You love your close friends. Love: one of those convoluted and ambiguous words that has always perplexed and annoyed me. I found this from Angel Kyodo Williams[22]: "The way I think of love most often these days is that love is space. It is developing our own capacity for spaciousness within ourselves to allow others to be as they are."

February 2020. I am dining at an Ethiopian restaurant in Jena with Anna and her friends. They are young people, all in their 30s. Smart and idealistic. I feel this as a true sharing, a trust that develops among us as we talk about zero-waste, biking and costly 300-dollar helmets, the dismantling of the Berlin Wall. How East Germans were forced to shoot their own countrymen fleeing across the wall, and if it was discovered that their shots intentionally missed, they were imprisoned. That East Germans were given their professions and so denied the opportunity to pursue their dreams, dreams that many of us take for granted. We eat from two large platters (no private plates), and split the bill six ways.

***

    I think about all the food and holidays we (my family and all of Nasrin's friends) shared with Nasrin. And not just the food, the cooking and the recipes, but the stories and ideas. I met many of Nasrin's friends over meals. Occasionally I would be on the East Hill for site visits, driving right past Terrace View so of course I'd stop in to say hello to Nasrin. *Here!* Nasrin would say, opening the refrigerator, and I'd protest, but no. *I'll heat it up right now. You have a few minutes!* How those delicious snacks made my work day more manageable.

    With Nasrin I shared plums, peaches, tomatoes, garlic, cucumbers, and she: prepared foods, clothes, makeup, and perfume. She just loved fresh plums and cooked the most delicious chicken and plum dish. We discussed our kid(s) and her grandson. This is characteristic of friendships among women. And there are other things that one shares with close friends: books, writing, traveling experiences. But for all of us, most of all, in one way or another, we let each other talk. We listened. We cared. We tried to troubleshoot and we tried to console. We talked about our jobs, our professions, our health, our families, our houses, our kids, and our futures, and our fears. We Moms are always thinking about our kids. And when we had deep wounds, our friends were there, and they are here, to thin the wounds, to take the edge off of a hard day and to make life more manageable.

    I have found no other affirmation more welcome than a friend who can stand up and support you when you know your bond with your husband has come unequivocally undone. This is a point that can't be argued: *I need to leave or my soul will die.* I can imagine Nasrin thinking that, and how grateful she was for the women who knew and supported her when she first moved to Iliad. I too, know how that felt from a dear friend: no judgement, just a full-hearted generosity.

Divorce can be transformative: a woman starts as a quiet, shrinking violet: *Yes Honey, when would you like dinner? Is the house clean enough?* to the: *Get out of my way, I have people to take care of, and nothing, damnit, is going to stop me.* Despite the xenophobia, the government ready to expel her, her lack of English, the unaccepted Iranian college degree, her poverty, Nasrin leapt forward.

I don't think she ever looked back.

Nasrin: planner, entrepreneur; she was fiercely independent and she had to be: a single mom, no local family, in a country whose people were encouraged to be hostile to Iranians. Nasrin acknowledged it, but let it go: she had too many other obligations, and when you're a single parent, you do everything, and mostly, you do everything alone.

When she was diagnosed with cancer Nasrin changed her diet – although she had a pretty darn healthy diet. She regularly attended meditation and she walked. Nasrin was willing to try anything and had no fear in that regard. She wanted to learn how to swim, and how to bike. I never got the chance to teach her.

There were things I wish I had said to Nasrin: how I admired how she pulled off the single working mom gig with wit and grit. How she defied all the stereotypes. She created a life for herself, and gathered together a group of women who became her family.

There were surprising things that *The Good Moms* said that I hadn't anticipated or was unable to articulate. It's a comfort to share the work of grief as you try to reconcile the death of a good person. We all wanted to declare *I was Nasrin's closest friend!* and each of us was, at one time or another. We all felt this need, and certainly near the end, to protect her.

"Life will break you," Louise Erdrich says in *The Painted Drum*.[23] "Nobody can protect you from that, and living alone won't either, for solitude will also break you with its yearning. You have to love. You have to feel. It is the reason you are here on earth. You are here to risk your heart. You are here to be swallowed up. And when it happens that you are broken, or betrayed, or left, or hurt, or death brushes near, let yourself sit by an apple tree and listen to the apples falling all around you in heaps, wasting their sweetness. Tell yourself you tasted as many as you could."

Nasrin and I would walk together occasionally, but we never ran together, so I was surprised when she called me in November 2018 announcing her desire to run the *Turkey Trot* on Thanksgiving Day. I asked her if she ever ran.

No, but I can walk 7 miles.

Running is different from walking, I said. I have run since my twenties.

I still want to go. I want to do something for myself, that's mine.

Thanksgiving morning, November 22, 2018, came into being as a bitingly cold day – the kind of day where you want to sit in front of a wood-burning stove and read. The race was to start at nine. At eight I called Nasrin hoping she had changed her mind. Temperatures were below 20. The wind was substantial.

I met Nasrin at Iliad High School, the first time I had been back since losing my job. We signed in and donated ten dollars to *Loaves and Fishes.* This was part of why she chose this run: this opportunity to help someone less fortunate. We assessed the free bagels and other food, stretched a little and glanced at the route on a large board; the route was convoluted and only partially followed roads. Eh, we decided: *We'll just follow the crowd.*

At nine when the cow bell rang, we *followed the crowd*. The run started behind the high school, towards the route 13 entrance, then up a steep rocky path. Nasrin and I ascended the hill on our hands and knees. Then up to Sunrise, onto Remington. I would say we weren't entirely prepared for this run: we brought no water. So when Nasrin said, *I'm thirsty*, I ran to a yard nearby that had an abundance of pristine snow, scooped some up, and gave it to Nasrin. *It's not the worst thing to put in your body,* I told her.

People kept galloping past us. There was one man running alone and he joined us, luckily so because by the time we got to Stewart Park, we had lost the pack. We were no longer running on roads, but paths, and the blowing snow obscured the footsteps of those in front of us. Our friend, Carl, a CU scientist, said he knew the route, that he'd completed the run several times. Still, we all hunted for footprints. We ran right along the lake at Stewart Park, and crossed parts of the park that I had never been to. The wind kept blowing hard. Carl, it turned out, was a biochemist. When we heard that, Nasrin and I looked at each other, both thinking the same thing. We told Carl we knew some very bright recently minted female biochemists who might be returning to Iliad. *Sure*, he said, *Give them my name*. Before the race's end, we understood that amoebas – even tiny single-celled amoebas – could communicate with one another. Amazing, I thought. Why hadn't I known that?

We stopped twice for side aches. Nasrin's.

The run was 5.5 miles long and we finished in 84 minutes. Of the 200 registered runners, Nasrin and I tied for 198th place[24]. It was the coldest Turkey Trot in the 46 years that the race existed. Fourteen degrees.

That night, as usual, my boyfriend, Mike, and I went to Sorayya's and Naeem's for Thanksgiving dinner, then to Nasrin's for dessert. Once again, Nasrin made an elaborate turkey dinner and pies. Yelena's, Carole's and Susan's families were there (as they often were), and whatever family Nasrin had visiting from Iran, and other friends.

There were things that I never got around to doing with Nasrin. She wanted to learn how to swim and how to cycle; cycling especially, but then there was Zahara's and Adam's wedding, the chemo, and as Nasrin regained her strength, she moved to Boston. I regret not taking her cycling with me, which is one of my greatest pleasures, and I had hoped it would be for her too. There are other regrets – like not telling her how much I admired her – as there always are when one passes. I wanted to talk to her about Michael Pollan's *How to Change Your Mind* [25]: psychedelic drugs used as a tool not only for mind expansion, but for reducing end-of-life anxiety.

This is what Headspace[26] says about regret. Regret is a focus on what could have been, "wanting things to have been different." We know we can't change the past, but we "can have influence on what happens in our minds. We need to give the mind time to unfold and change the unhelpful patterns in the mind. This encourages one to cultivate a sense of forgiveness in ourselves, and peace of mind to let go of certain thoughts."

We just never get to everything. But we did get to some things.

Once when I was feeling really low after losing my job, Nasrin and Susan and I went on Match.com. We made a few risqué comments about the men and their photos, and laughed about the very small things they wanted. All in good humor. We went out a few times on dates and returned with stories to tell. During that period I came over to Nasrin's with a bottle of Lucus Vineyards wine. *This is good wine, right?* I said. *It comes in a cobalt blue bottle.* We drank the whole bottle and talked, and laughed about a CU professor she was dating, and several Guthrie clients (whose breast X-rays she had taken), who had asked her out. The night of the cobalt blue wine bottle, I fell asleep on her living room floor, woke around five, drove home and when I got there, I found that the kids had locked me out. Luckily there was a ladder nearby and my bedroom window was open. And there was Nasrin's mysterious first love (high school) from Iran, whom she met later in life, twice in her 50s, and with great anticipation. They traveled together. He was unfortunately "not sufficiently evolved" to be with such an independent and intelligent woman.

Lastly, about three or four weeks before Nasrin died, Mike and I went over to Nasrin's to watch a movie with her. Adam, Zahara and Oliver went out to eat. Of course, Zahara left fresh pizza for us.

Nasrin was wearing a yellow summer dress: *Look at this dress*, she said, twirling around. *A two-dollar dress!* and even though she was rail-thin by then, she looked elegant and exotic. It evoked the first time we met, back in 1997: an enchanting woman who grasped the essence of life, and who wasn't going to let go of it. The dress was the yellow of black-eyed Susan's, a native plant that attracts beneficial insects. The color gave her eyes an even deeper brown color. She was light and free and content. The movie we watched – and we didn't know the storyline before we came – was about an immigrant woman who raised a daughter all alone, against all odds, and how that daughter was soon to be without her mother.

Our children are the living messages we send to a future we will never see ... Will we rob them of their destiny? Will we rob them of their dreams? No, we will not do that. ee cummings.

I., New York, May 5, 2021

Afterward: July 25, 2021

Two years after Nasrin's passing, I e-mailed those I had interviewed asking participants how their lives had changed, if they had other thoughts on the issues we had talked about during their interview. Only one individual responded saying that she had nothing new to add. People move on, and I understood that (and maybe not have recalled their interview), but I had immersed myself in this book for two years, starting with the interviews, most of which took place face-to-face. How had I changed? For me, writing the book was transformative.

First, the interview process mandated that I become a more skillful listener; thoughtful listening is a technique that I am still working on and will always be working on. I deliberately stop myself now when I am in a conversation, and if I'm on the ball that day, I'll remind myself not to interrupt or think ahead, and to listen without assumptions, otherwise I am not listening. If I am patient, then I will inspect my ideas and opinions before sharing them. Everyone benefits from a more thoughtful conversation. The phase *being present* used to perplex me, but I have a deeper sense of what it means now. When I can be present with another person, I am a better person and a better friend.

How else has my life changed? I have devoted more time to exploring my own spirituality, or simply: what does my life mean to me *every day?* I used to equate spirituality with religion, and believed it had the trappings of superstition, rigidity, ritual, misogyny and war, but that perspective has changed. I've taken the time to read books and explore podcasts on Buddhism and try other types of meditation. And although I don't completely understand the concepts of wise speech, wise thought, and wise action, the notions make more sense to me and

I am trying to consciously implement them in my daily life. This is important for how I want to live my life.

Covid has had an impact too. Because the start of my job was delayed two months in 2020, I was able to put more effort into the book than I would have otherwise. Because the restaurants, breweries and coffee shops were closed, I spent a lot of time walking and thinking about writing, love and friendship. I reconsidered some of my habits. Did I want to change the non-productive, unskillful and sometimes negative thought patterns? I sure did. As Ben is fond of saying: "Twenty-one days and you have a habit."

I did take to heart what many had advised: *Don't keep putting off what you want to do in life*, and I would add: *Or be who you want to be. Now.* By chance I saw a documentary on Minimalism, which in a sense I had been practicing for years with respect to my clothes and books, but after some research, this way of living triggered more questions, and then permission to part with other things, the mantra being *Use things, Love people*. The battle against saving things for future use or for sentimental reasons was more easily won as I armed myself with hard facts and stories of people who were evangelical about their material proliferation. After all, why spend time on things rather than on myself, my family, or friends?

The last change was in April 2021 when Anna gave birth to a baby boy. It was a difficult birth and a long recovery. I was in Germany once again (July 2021) this time helping Anna get back on her feet – literally: we walked every day, sometimes two or three times-a-day. The baby had been born two years later, and almost to the hour of Nasrin's passing. And as I sit here, a first-time grandmother, I hear Nasrin from the past (although sometimes she is still very much in the present) advising me: *Pat, do something for yourself. Keep something for yourself*. And I want to say to her: *See Nasrin. I have. And I will.*

References

Part 1: Nasrin

1. Map derived from Image:Iran topo en.jpg, original image by en:User:Captain Blood, CC BY-SA 3.0, https://commons.wikimedia.org/w/index.php?curid=3006920.

2. Kahneman, Daniel (Http://www.bcwm.com/he-undressed-the-maid-himself/) accessed January 2020.

3. headspace.com, see section on stress.

Part II: Immigrants, Immigration and Iran

1. https://worldpopulationreview.com/state-rankings/native-american-population, accessed December 2019.

2. Deparle, Jason, "The Open Borders Trap," *New York Times*, March 8, 2020.

3. justin@optimallivingdaily.com sent October 10, 2019.

4. Nazario, Sonia, "What Part of Illegal Don't you Understand," February 19, 2020.

5. Chomsky, Noam, *Yugoslavia, Peace, War and Dissolution*, edited by Davor Dzalto, PM Press, Oakland, California, 2018.

6. https://www.britannica.com/event/Bosnian-War, accessed March 2020.

7. https://en.wikipedia.org/wiki/Iran; most of this section is based on this entry; accessed December 2019.

8. Personal communication with Carolyn, April 21, 2020.

9. https://en.wikipedia.org/wiki/Amol, accessed December 2019.

10. Encyclopedia Britannica, Britannica.com/place/Amol, accessed December 2019.

11. itto.org/Iran/city/amol-mazandaran/, accessed December 2019.

12. unsplash.com/slphotos/amol%2c-iran), accessed December 2019.

13. Polk, William R. *Understanding Iran: Everything you need to know from Persia to the Islamic Republic, from Cyrus to Ahmadinejad,* Macmillian, New York 2009.

14. https://www.irantravelingcenter.com/deserts-of-iran/, accessed December 2019.

15. https://en.wikipedia.org/wiki/List_of_mountains_in_Iran, accessed December 2019.

16. https://en.wikipedia.org/wiki/Mount_Damavand, accessed December 2019.

17. https://en.wikipedia.org/wiki/Hassan_Rouhani Hassan, accessed December 2019.

18. Democracy Now, December 23, 2019 radio broadcast https://www.democracynow.org/.

19. Radio Farda, *2019-2020 Iranian Protests*, https://en.wikipedia.org/wiki/2019%E2%80%9320_Iranian_protests.

20. Radio Farda, *Iran Still Among the Lowest in Human Freedom Index*, https://en.radiofarda.com/a/iran-lowest-in-human-freedom-index/30334206.html

21. Wright, Robin "Ghost Towers*,"* *The New Yorker*, October 21, 2019.

22. https://en.wikipedia.org/wiki/Qasem_Soleimani, Qasem Solemani, accessed April 2020.

23. ABC news, November 11, 1979: https://www.youtube.com/watch?v=A8bC1DEYbI4

24. Farber, David, *Taken Hostage: The Iran Hostage Crisis and America's First Encounter with Radical Islam,* Princeton, New Jersey, Princeton University Press, 2005.

25. https://coup53.com/ *Coup 53 Documentary*, accessed February 2020.

26. Carolyn personal communication, April 21, 2020.

27. wikipedia.org/wiki/Mohammad_Mosaddegh, accessed February 2020.

28. https://en.wikipedia.org/wiki/2,500-year_celebration_of_the_Persian_Empire, accessed February 2020.

29. https://en.wikipedia.org/wiki/Executive_Order_12170, accessed February 2020.

30. https://timeline.com/1979-hostage-crisis-iranians-in-us-lived-in-fear-of-deportation-97c450f3b7b3 , accessed February 2020.

Part III: Reflections After a Death

1. Henry, Joe, "Welcoming Flies at the Picnic," *On Being* podcast, accessed January 2020.

2. Rowson, John, "Our Souls, Systems and Society," *On Being* podcast, accessed January 2020.

3. Williams, Angel Kyodo, "The Spiritual Aspect of Social Change," *On Being* podcast, accessed January 2020.

4. Hempton, Gordon, "Sounds of Silence," *On Being* podcast accessed March 2020.

5. Payne, Katy, "In the Presence of Elephants and Whales," *On Being* podcast accessed March 2020.

6. Sacks, Oliver, *Musicophilia, Tales of Music and the Brain*, Vintage Books, Random House, Inc, New York, 2007.

7. Coyne, George, "Asteroids, Stars and the Love of God," *On Being* podcast accessed March 2020.

8. Kubler Ross, *On Death and Dying*, 1969, Macmillan Company, New York.

9. McInerny, Nora, *We don't move on from grief, we move forward with it*, TED Woman, 2018.

10. Bonanno, George, *The Other Side of Sadness: What the New Science of Bereavement Tells Us About Life After Loss*, Basic Books, 2019.

11. headspace.com, see section on grieving.

12. Naipaul, V.S., "Grief, A writer reckons with loss," *The New Yorker*, January 6, 2020.

13. Payne, Katy, "In the Presence of Elephants and Whales," *On Being* podcast accessed March 2020.

14. https://www.nst.com.my/lifestyle/pulse/2019/02/460406/

valentines-day-lovers-throng%E2%80%A6-museum-broken-relationships;

For VHS tape, see
https://books.google.com/books?id=g9P3DQAAQBAJ&pg=PT105&lpg=PT105&dq=Museum+of+broken+relationships+VHS+tape+marriage&source=bl&ots=RaNY6lv7Q5&sig=ACfU3U2volkv9EWppbthLcomq5hjPd2UTw&hl=en&sa=X&ved=2ahUKEwjxr5647uznAhVBYTUKHUTbDnEQ6AEwAHoECAoQAQ#v=onepage&q=Museum%20of%20broken%20relationships%20VHS%20tape%20marriage&f=false.

15. https://oldpodcast.com/, "Optimal Daily Living" podcast, accessed April 4, 2019.

16. Schjeldahl, Peter, "77 Sunset Me, Notes on an ending," *The New Yorker*, December 23, 2019.

17. https://www.imdb.com/title/tt0734609/, Twilight Zone, *One for the Angels,* video accessed January 2020.

18. Jones, Maggie, "The Long Goodbye," *The New York Times Magazine*, 2019 https://www.nytimes.com/2019/12/19/magazine/home-funeral.html, December 22, 2019.

19. Doughty, Caitlin, "Death Becomes Her*," Call Your Girlfriend* podcast, October 11, 2019, https://www.callyourgirlfriend.com/.

20. https://journals.sagepub.com/doi/10.1177/0013916506295573, accessed January 2020.

21. Steindl-Rast, David, "How to Be Grateful in Every Moment, But Not for Everything"*, On Being* podcast, accessed January 2020.

22. Williams, Angel Kyodo, "The Spiritual Aspect of Social Change," *On Being* podcast, accessed January 2020.

23. Erdrich, Louise, *The Painted Drum*, Harper Perennial, New York, 2006.

24. https://fingerlakesrunners.org/wp-content/uploads/2017/11/Turkey-Run-2018-Results.pdf, Look on the list: Nasrin is #62.

25. Pollan, Michael, *How to Change Your Mind,* Penguin Press, London, 2018.

26. www.headscape.com, see section on regret, accessed April 2020.

Appendix: The Interviews

The interviews begin with Sarah, the only individual who did not know Nasrin. Then Hashem's, Nasrin's brother, follows along with interviews of friends from the younger generation, and finally interviews of friends from Nasrin's generation. The people I interviewed included a nurse, a midwife, a nurse practitioner, a clinical social worker, an office administrator, a grant writer, a novelist, a food entrepreneur and musician, another musician, a grad student, an officiant, an holistic healer, an online teacher, a statistician and business owner, a businessman, two anthropologists, two oncologists, three PhD chemists, and many moms and their children.

The interviews are in the following order:

1. Sarah   121
2. Hashem   124
3. Hannah   126
4. Ben   129
5. Anna   133
6. April   135
7. Adam   140
8. Zahara   144
9. Yasamin   149
10. Julia and Shiv 154
11. Marie   157
12. Alice   161
13. Zahara   165
14. Sorayya   175
15. Zhila   181
16. Carolyn   188

17. Virginia 195
18. Susan 202
19. Zahara 208
20. Noni 211
21. Debbie 215
22. Sue 221

Acknowledgements 228

1. Sarah, phone interview, 7-15-2020.

Sarah was the only person I interviewed who did not know Nasrin. A friend connected us, and I include her interview because she gave a sense of what it is like be a young Iranian immigrant in the US in 1979.

Tell me about yourself.

I live in New York City, I am clinical social worker, mostly work in the neurology in the areas of Parkinson's and megaloblastic cases, pediatric neurology and care coordination. In the evening I have a small private practice. Before that I was an elementary school teacher, and taught in college. I came to the US August of '79. August 13. My dad was a Communist, born in Azerbaijani. His dad died young. During WW II there was the option of staying in Azerbaijani or crossing into Iran, and he came to Iran. His first language was Turkish, and his mother born was born in St Petersburg. We're of mixed heritage. During the war he worked in a factory sewing Russian uniforms. He moved to US initially because he was very unhappy with the Shah monarchy. In 1953 he was pro-Mossadegh. There was a CIA-backed coup in 1953. Roosevelt had responsibility here, Iran had an opportunity to become democratic, but British Petroleum and American interests got in the way.

My father's brother was a big drinker, and he was messing up, so my Dad went back to Iran. He was a leading socialist communist, and he stayed with his biological Mom. She had been divorced, and a single parent, nurse administrator. My dad had integrity, he got married. I (Sarah) was born when he was 42, she was 37. It was not a typical marriage – she was a single woman working on her own in Tehran. She went to the beach, did not practice Islam, and celebrated the New Year. She wasn't very Muslim or Islamic. In the 70s things started changing, and my Dad wanted to come back to US. My Mom did not want come because her Dad was here (Iran) and she was attached to him. We stayed but things kept changing, and he wanted to go. There were the Revolutionaries. Machine guns fired at our house. My Dad's sister worked in the government. Everyone was getting arrested and getting stopped on the street. She got arrested for wearing a mini skirt. She could not hold her tongue. 'You don't know how to stop talking,' she was told. My uncle got arrested because he worked for the government (The Shah), and we knew he was going to get arrested so we hid him in the house. You lived a normal life but the people against the government had an arsenal that they would use against you. My uncle was in Evin Prison, a notorious prison.

How did you leave Iran?

One of my Dad's best friends, Mark, worked at the embassy. They used to hang out. Mark said, 'You have to leave.' He got us green cards and we left over night with a suitcase. 'You have to leave, and you have to leave now,' he said. Before that my Dad was a big traveler and always came to the states. He sent most of younger siblings to the US, and put them through college, always traveling back and forth.

How did you feel about leaving?

I was in third grade and I didn't know what was happening. It was hard to say to goodbye to my grandfather. Each of us had a suitcase and a box--things from my grandfather. That was the box that was lost.

I believed we arrived on the 13th of August, my birthday was on 22nd, and I started school 28th. I did not speak English. I was mute for three months and did not talk to parents or anyone. I would withdraw a lot, and retreat. Then I started talking.

Where did you live?

We lived in Chicago and New York.

Have you ever had any desire to return to Iran?

I have. I was a Wild Child. I finished school early and drove across country and had my first apartment when I was 16. In college I did research at De Paul University in Chicago. As a history major, I worked with a professor writing a history of Near Eastern Communism in 1859. My father said, 'You go to demonstrations. You should go to Iran.' I shaved my head so I looked like a guy and went because there was an interview component of the research that the professor was doing. I went for three weeks, it was strange, being a traveler, and I didn't realize I couldn't get a hotel room. It was a strange trip. Iranian women are really beautiful: they pay a lot of attention to makeup and clothing.

Did you connect with any relatives?

No. I don't know anyone there anymore.

Do you have any desire to go back now?

It's not on my list of places to visit.

What was it like when you first got to the US?

There was a lot of 'Go home you fucking Iranian.' By the kids and the teachers. It hurt, it was really, really awful and bad. There's a comforting understanding that we do share the same practices, but different practices and perspectives give you a different lens. We have this unique human curiosity and to have it squashed so very early.

2. Hashem, in person, 6-28-2019, translated by M., Hashem's son.

I interviewed Hashem two months after Nasrin's death. The interview itself was rushed (Hashem was returning to Iran), and not as spontaneous as I would have liked because of translation complications, but it gives a glimpse of Nasrin that no one else had access to.

Tell me a little about yourself.

I am Hashem, 57 years-old and grew up in the city of Amol, Mazandaran, population around 500,000, between the mountain and the sea. Because of the location, everyone comes to our city for vacation. A lot of farmers are there, and the city makes stuff: cars, appliances. It is a very old city.

What did your parents do?

Mom brought up five children, Dad was the owner of properties to rent, and he had farms, and ships. He was a merchant.

Please describe Nasrin.

She was a humble kid. She worried about the rest of the family and their success. She didn't bother anyone. She did give advice, even as a kid. And she didn't like liars. Everyone had so much respect for her even as a kid. She went to three years of college and she was the only one. She loved school and studying and was made for it. She worked for a year in the schools – inspecting schools for kids' health. She pushed me to go to school. All schools were boys or girls only.

Why did she leave Iran?

She didn't want to leave, but many did. She got married and moved to California in 1981. Then they moved to Iliad because her husband got a job in Iliad.

What is your favorite memory of Nasrin?

Me and my son, eight years ago, saw Nasrin here with her success. She did everything by herself. She had four siblings, and growing up everyone was close. I was the closest, but Nasrin was a person who loved everyone and wished for everyone's success, even for all family and friends. She sent money to help us, and she gave money to the homeless.

When did she come back to visit?

When she could afford it. Zahara was four years-old.

Why didn't she return to Iran?

Because of Zahara, and because she couldn't picture herself living anywhere else other than Iliad.

3.Hannah, phone interview, 1-29-2020.

Hi Hannah. Can you tell me a little about yourself?

I was born in Iliad, New York, and currently live in New York City. I just finished a free-school and I am now certified as a nurse midwife, and I'm pregnant and expecting my first baby in March. I still work as a labor and delivery nurse. My husband is Adam and we live in Chelsea and he works for a mobile bank. We're excited to be parents.

Nice. How do you like living in New York City?

We love it. It's grown on me. When I first got here I didn't know how long I could take it, but now I don't think I could live anywhere else. We've been here eight years and we're trying to move to a bigger apartment. We have two Siamese cats and you may hear them in the background.

Do you remember when you first met Nasrin?

It was probably when I was in kindergarten.

Is that when you met Zahara?

My Mom knew Kumi (Noni's Mom) through architecture work – Kumi had designed a blueprint for my Mom and that's how we met Maia's family, and through them, I met Nasrin and Zahara. I remember going to a birthday party of Zahara's – I have pictures of it – in kindergarten. They both lived on West Hill.

Did you go to Nasrin's house much?

I went there a lot, especially as I got older. I had more of a direct friendship with Zahara in middle school, instead of play dates.

Did you remember going on sleepovers?

I do! One specific memory was Nasrin would make flan a lot. I never had flan before and I thought it was the most amazing thing. It's like a custard. Another memory is that Zahara and I would ask Nasrin to curl our hair and it would look terrible every time. I would sleep over just to get her to do it, and it would never look quite like we thought it would. We'd go out in the morning and have to hide our hair.

Did Nasrin ever talk to you about Iran?

No, not really.

How her death affected you?

Her death has definitely affected me – I haven't had a lot of close people in my life pass away. It makes you think about your relationship with your own mother, how you would feel if your own mother passed away. I felt optimistic when Nasrin was first diagnosed. How could something like that happen to a wonderful person? It's a loss.

How would you describe Nasrin?

Generous is the first word that comes to mind. Anytime you were in her house, she would make you feel at home and offer you food, and she would ask about me and my family. She was always giving me and my mom gifts, and for no occasion.

Would you describe yourself as a spiritual person?

Definitely. I didn't grow up with a religion, but spirituality was part of my upbringing. My parents both had an Indian spiritual teacher and I watched my mom meditate. We grew up with a belief in god, but not tied to a religion. Spiritualism is important to me.

Has her death affected your sense of spirituality?

My spirituality affects the way I feel about the dead and dying. I felt a deep sense of loss. For sure, I think about Nasrin and I feel her presence. It doesn't feel like she's gone.

Is that how you mourn?

Yes. The last time I went to Zahara's house, the first time since Nasrin passed away, I felt special being in that space and I definitely felt her presence.

Is there anything else about Nasrin, that you've incorporated into your life?

Just being an example of such generosity, and it makes you want to be like that. I think about her as I am about to become a mother. She was the most dedicated mother.

Anything else you want to add?

The last time I saw Nasrin, it was in Boston, and I spent a couple of days at Zahara's and Adam's, just hanging out with them. Nasrin looked really good, we had some food and she made us tea. And we were just hanging out and playing with Oliver. She was really happy to be with her grandson and feeling good. I think about that day. That's how I want to remember Nasrin.

4. Ben, in person, 10-20-2019.

Tell me a little bit about yourself.

I'm a student studying for the GRE, the test to get into graduate school. I volunteer in the community as a youth mentor and a few other things, doing writing and tutoring. I should play fewer video games. I'm just starting to read again, and I exercise, four times-a-week. I meditate every day for health reasons. I'm in recovery from an emotional condition.

What is your field of study?

I have an Associate of Science in psychology and Bachelor of Arts in human development.

Do you remember the first time that you met Nasrin?

I don't remember.

Can you describe Nasrin?

I don't know how valuable my description will be but she was a stoic figure who was very formal and polite, but at the same time, she wasn't stuck up, and she'd be the sort of person that you could discuss complicated topics with, and she would she wouldn't just humor you, she would dive into them and be a good friend. She was in some ways a motherly icon. I would go to her house before school and she would give me all these little gifts. She would wait on us and let me watch TV. The atmosphere was cordial, not uptight or pretentious.

Do you remember how old you were when you went to Nasrin's house?

Third or fifth grade. I didn't like her dog, I will say that.

Hershey. Why?

I don't like small dogs because small dogs tend to be very noisy. As such with hers. But I put up with it.

Do you remember her coming to our house during the holidays?

I do have more of a vague memory there because my connection was through you, and through Zahara, who was friends with my sister, Anna. She was a very steady woman, steady gaze, and would always welcome me, suggesting an extended family member.

Has her death affected you?

There's no doubt it's affected me, just from what I would call mental shock waves. Otherwise, I know I feel that I didn't know her very well, and it would have been nice to know her better. Mom, you were great friends so you knew her at a much deeper level. She was like an aunt.

Did you know what she went through to make a successful life here?

As always, I am aware of some things that happened, but not everything. I learned in a class that during the Iranian Revolution that women were scapegoats for basically every faction, every party vilified women. Iran and the US didn't have great relations, to put it facetiously, especially after 9-11. There was discrimination, and on top of this, she raised a child who turned out very well. Zahara went to great colleges and is a very, very smart person who studied bio-chem. And thinking back on it, it was something that Nasrin was able to show me kindness, despite all the crap that she must have gotten from other people, and the fact that I'm Jewish, and was raised as a Jew, and how much more terrible the relations are between Iran and Israel than between the US and Iran. She didn't turn me into a category of evil because of my heritage.

After her death--have you thought about your own death, or differently about death?

There's no doubt when someone dies however close to me, it makes me think about mortality. 2017 was a bizarre year: before that year, mom, your father was the closest person to ever die and that was in 2005. In 2017 my (other) grandfather and my best friend's brother died, and some whom I knew with a degree or two of separation.

Do these deaths make you think more about your spirituality?

Not so much but they contribute to a view, in Western culture, a shining idea of death, because people are scared of it, and how reality doesn't matter if we put up walls, or have this police force, and so on. We're all mortal, we're all animals and we're part of the wild. We die just as other beings do. I'm just a little ashamed that I feel that in some ways positive, that I'm able to keep on going. You know? Whether that's a testament or an insult to those who died.

Ben, how do you mourn?

I'm not sure. I learned from school that there's no real set stages of mourning, despite some psychologists saying there are. It's very different for each person. It's further different for each person who has died, and their relationship to that person. So how do I mourn? I cried a few times and I flock to those alive and offer support. I can't justify a connection to god. To offer comfort and support to those alive, that's a concrete way of doing good. God is a very abstract sense of things and people, and to know a sense of god depends on how much I meditate. That's my belief.

Thank you. Would you like to say anything else?

I try my best not to go down a road that'll lead to pain and misery. It's easy to adopt Nietzsche and be nihilistic and such. It may feel right and it may feel good, but that's just a dead end. Similarly talking or thinking of one taking one's own life. It's weird it's, it's paradoxical but it never leads to anything of substance. Maybe these deaths have allowed us some wisdom to celebrate life more. Most intellectuals will agree we don't have any real proof of any of something divine, or if avatars exist. We all die, but you don't have to keep your eyes on death.

We don't have to have this fear of death and god that society inoculated in us, based on a Christian background. People pass on. I don't think that's in the end necessarily a terrible thing. We all pass on.

5. Anna, in person, 9-27-19.

Tell me about yourself.

I'm your daughter and I'm visiting after Isha's wedding. I live in Germany against the wishes of my mother (laughter), but I lived in Iliad for 10 years. I moved here when I was eight and left for college when I was 17. I'm a biochemist.

Do you remember the first time you met Nasrin?

Not really, but I was in 4th grade. We had just moved to C. Heights school, I had been in Northeast school before, but I hadn't made any friends and I was so I was so excited when Zahara called me up to play. I don't remember meeting Nasrin but obviously I must have. I vaguely remember the first time going to Hook Place.

Did you go to the Hook Place house often?

I was over there quite a bit for sleepovers and birthday parties. We weren't friends in middle school – I don't remember why – we must have had a fight. We were kind of friends in high school, but I was on the outside of things. Then you and Nasrin were friends. I remember sleeping over there, it must have been in 5th grade, and it was really hot, and only Nasrin's room had a fan, so we slept in her room. She must have slept on the couch or in Zahara's room.

Did you eat dinner there?

I ate there quite a bit. She didn't cook Iranian food – that started when I was older – she made more kid-friendly food for Zahara and her friends. Later on we had her Iranian food. It was really good.

Has her death made you think about your own death?

No – I'm quite a bit younger, and to me I think it's (death) is kind of unfathomable, and since I wasn't here to witness any of her last days, or witness her illness, it's unreal to me. I witnessed it only through you, or talking with Zahara.

Is there anything else you want to say about Nasrin as a person?

She liked to buy people gifts. She had a particular sense of style that she was committed to, not my style, but it's cool when people have a style and are unabashedly committed to it. Her style was TJ Max chic. She loved TJMax. Zahara always looked really chic: you can shop there if you're thin and dark. Her house looked nice because she could cull from TJ Max.

Nasrin was a good seamstress, and once let me and Zahara pick out fabric. I picked out the ugliest fabric – in retrospect, that was the right response (not suggesting another fabric) – and she sewed us pants, one for each of us.

Do you remember the red pants she made for Zahara?

No, but she must have made a lot of clothes for Zahara. Pajama pants. They were really cool, and not a small amount of work.

6. April, in person, 1-14-2020.

Tell me about yourself.

I grew up in Austin, Texas, and Albuquerque, and I moved to Iliad with my family in 2000. I went to college at Lawrence University in Wisconsin, then moved to New York City for a year. Now I'm back in Iliad, and I run a food stand at the farmer's market. I sing and play guitar.

How did you meet Nasrin?

It's a long, funny story. I went to a Catholic school in Austin called Sacred Heart, and one of my classmates, Anita (Virginia's daughter) came to Austin in the fourth grade. When I moved to Iliad, which is where Anita had grown up, she said you should contact these friends of mine, Zahara and Julia. I showed up here in eighth grade I didn't know anyone and I attached myself to Zahara and the others. They were welcoming and we quickly became friends. Then I met Nasrin. We would have sleepovers at the house on Hook Place. That was my first memory of Nasrin.

Can you describe the sleepovers?

The sleepovers. We were in eighth grade so it was all very silly. A really interesting part of my relationship with Nasrin was seeing how it changed over time as I grew up. But at that point understandably, she was parental to everyone and extremely warm and the house always smelled like great Persian spices. It was playful and free and there were lots of different friends. Some houses were stricter. Not Nasrin's. She seemed to trust us more than other parents. From the beginning she was extremely kind.

Did she ever talk to you about Iran?

She talked to my dad about Iranian politics. The kind of conversations we had were about her family and the culture clash between expectations and willingness or unwillingness meeting them.

She was in Iran during less fun times, but we did not talk about them. Maybe three months before she passed, Nasrin was seeing the same therapist I saw. They talked, I believe, about the family history, and the craziness associated with Nasrin's dad.

How has her death affected you?

It's hard. It affected me way more than I could have predicted. Being relatively younger, I've lost grandparents and friends to drugs, but this one's much harder because she was relatively young, and she's the one who I've known the longest. She was like a parent: I called her Mom and she called me Daughter. I think about her a lot. I'm assuming that's normal but for me what I noticed is we all had these moments at the funeral. She was such a rock. The life experiences that she's missing are really hard for me, like the fact that Zahara's pregnant and she won't meet her second grandchild, or meet Hannah's. She was thrilled for me (Farmer's Market) so that's kind of a hilarious point--when I thought I lost the food stand. I definitely felt that when the final agreement was signed it was a huge bummer, for her not to hear about it.

When someone passes and they say *I'm sorry for your loss:* this is the first one, it's more than a day-to-day loss. It's harder in the sense that you can't see someone, someone who I could reach out to. That's an incredible loss.

How do you mourn?

It's not always with people. One thing that helps is being in the space that I shared with that person. Her house. That's an ideal grieving space, and remembering all of it: the good and the bad, then keeping memories and letting them go simultaneously. Being in that space is helpful. I'm sure it's not easy for Zahara. It's been a longer process than I anticipated. But I guess that's relatively normal.

Has her death made you more spiritual in any sense?

I'm spiritual by nature, not necessarily in any religion. It's an interesting question because there's aspects of it that I don't like. I definitely have more questions after her passing. Zahara and I both talked about how Nasrin had a lot of really positive experiences that were other-worldly, indicating she was going to be okay. For me, the angelic signs and Oliver signs are important.

When you say she was going to be okay you mean Zahara or Nasrin?

Nasrin. Zahara has these pretty crazy intense stories.

Would you like to talk about them?

Sure. I don't know the context of why but Nasrin was in a church. I don't remember if it was Catholic. She was sitting in the very back and at one point the preacher or someone was speaking up at the front looked at her and said, "Please come up here." He said that in front of everyone and while she was up front, he said: "I know you're really worried, but you're going be okay. You're going to be a beacon, or a story to inspire other people." Who knows? We take things more literally whereas I'm less literal in that sense. Then she had this other story: she had a green piece of fabric on her wrist, as a bracelet that someone had given her. I don't remember the significance of the green fabric, but it had to do with being Muslim, a spiritual leader. The fabric is good luck and several times in the middle of the night she would wake, and the fabric would be outstretched under her shirt, where she had scars from surgeries, which I think you can read into that in several ways, but she saw that as a positive Those things were hard for us but it would be okay, for the three of us.

You've learned from Nasrin.

A lot of things that you don't realize until the person's gone. Not that I didn't experience a lot while she was alive. What's the right word? She was so warm and caring from the first moment. Zahara and I've always been very close, but I don't know when exactly Nasrin became like a mom and I became like a daughter. I feel like I gained more, and I think being an adult now, as an eighth grader you don't know anything. It's interesting being adult, to be able to see certain things. At the funeral we talked about Iran, that it is supposed to be our enemy in some way, shape or form. When you're a kid you don't know or acknowledge that, not that I see Iranians now as the enemy, but cultural politics don't play a part. I learned a lot about myself through both of them. For instance, you assume everyone had a school 'like my high school.' From Nasrin and Zahara, I was exposed to their culture and their food.

Nasrin's spirituality was always very multifaceted. She wasn't loud about it. I learned about the ability to be open and warm from her, and ease of being, and ease of being a parent.

You may have already answered this question, but what was it that drew you to her?

I was drawn to Zahara, then Nasrin. I think it is a pretty weird coincidence that I met another girl (Anita) in elementary school – they were from India – and I could see her mom and Nasrin getting along really well. They were very similar. So I guess as a child in eighth grade, her warmth, and especially being new to Iliad, and not knowing a single person. I grew up in a close-knit neighborhood where there were kids my age, their parents were like my parents, so that part had a similar comforting feeling.

Why did you move to Iliad?

My mom grew up in Rochester and her family's there – that's the short answer. My brother was struggling in Austin but we visited for the summer and ended up staying. Every summer we would get a cabin on the lake and go to the Adirondacks; the summer we moved, we were supposed to go back to Austin the following week. That's pretty much why I'm here – not because of Cornell.

Do you want to say anything else about Nasrin?

It's interesting that I knew them since eighth grade and now I'm in my early 30s. It's great to see how our relationship changed but also how the Zahara-Nasrin relationship changed. I have a distinct memory of how Nasrin would say Zahara's name. When we were kids, it was: *Zahara, stop doing that*, or you know, more like a parent, then as she got older, it just became – we all became – equal. You become friends.

I've noticed that with my kids.

Everything subtly changes.

7. Adam., in person, 12-8-2019.

Tell me a little bit about yourself.

I'm originally from California but spent a lot of time in Oregon. I met Zahara in graduate school while we were both in San Diego. I met her mom soon after, even before we started dating because Nasrin was such a big part of her life. We ultimately got married, and Nasrin was my mother-in-law. I'm a scientist working in discovery and development. Specifically, I'm a computational chemist. I develop new drugs for untreated health conditions.

Do you like your job?

It's exciting. You can be creative and make or engineer something that nobody else has done before.

You mentioned meeting Zahara when you were in graduate school.

Yes, then we got married in 2016, in July. Nasrin had started chemo before that. She lived with us in 2017, about a month before our son was born in August 2017. She came out earlier and then we never let her leave. She helped us learn to be parents.

How?

Neither Zahara or I had any younger siblings or much experience at all with infants so she showed us everything from diaper changing to calming them down, how to cuddle and hold them. Everything.

She lived with you in Boston.

Yes and spending some time in Iliad but mostly Boston. So Nasrin really bonded with Oliver. I feel like she was a second mom to Oliver.

Did she ever tell you any stories about Iran or about her life in Iran?

She told some stories, mostly she talked about her family. She was a big family person. She would talk about her Dad being extremely kind and generous, like she (Nasrin) was, and her mom as well. He would give to the people in their village who needed things. Her dad was some sort of businessman.

Did she ever tell you the story of how the INS raided her house?

No, she didn't talk to me about those things. Mostly talked about good memories of Iran and her family.

And you were thinking of going to Iran?

At some point we'd like to go and see her family, and then for Oliver, to learn a more about his heritage.

You had planned to go but then you decided not to go. Why?

We traveled with Oliver and decided it was too far to go.

Were you worried about the political situation?

We know many people who have gone, and it's been fine.

How would you describe Nasrin?

The best description is just endless generosity and kindness towards people, and empathy. She was a very good role model in that way. She had a lot of excitement for everything in life and even doing things that most people wouldn't – like chores – it didn't bring her down at all. She enjoyed doing everything.

And while she was living with you, did she cook for you?

Yes and we tried to convince her to relax and rest but she was always sneaking into the kitchen and cooking us delicious things. Of course we were thankful, but we just wanted her to take care of herself.

What have you learned about yourself from living with Nasrin? How have you developed as an individual?

I've definitely thought about how I approach different situations. Nasrin was good at understanding people and how they were feeling about something, and it's helped me to be more empathetic. I think more actively about what I want to do with my life. Seeing somebody's life come to an end you realize that it doesn't go on forever, but when you're younger you think it does, that you can do whatever forever. She certainly helped me to be a better parent, and to raise Oliver in a way where he feels really loved and cared for.

How has her death affected you?

I was brought up atheist, but I think that there's something more out there. That seems strange that we'd have all of these conscious minds and thoughts, and that they just go away. I'm hopeful that there's something more to it.

Would say that her death has you reflect on your spiritual side?

Yes.

Has that affected your thoughts on bringing up Oliver?

Yes. We're not going to push any specific religion on him, but we want him to feel that the world is a wonderful place and part of that is that there might be something for people to go to, or they may remain in some way in the world, after they leave. That's how we explained why he doesn't see his grandmother. He talks about her every day.

Nasrin's death: has it made you think more about your own death?

Yes. Hopefully that's still a long way away. But it reminds you that you don't want to waste your life because you really only have the present moment. We're always planning for the future – too much – and forget to live in the present moment. Nasrin reminds you that you'd like to make the most of whatever you do have. I was worried about the future. Planning for it. I've tried to catch myself, and remember that Oliver's only this age for a short while. So play with him, and be in the moment.

Do you want to say anything else about Nasrin?

She was just a unique person. I've never met anybody so generous. And so kind and also was so good at reading social world. She'd meet a person and have an excellent sense of that person and in no time. She also had an excellent sense of what would improve life; I've never seen anybody who actively and proactively thought about how to help others around her. She had a huge network of people who loved her. Knowing her has made me think that we'd like to build a similar network. We have to be kind, generous, and understanding.

How do you mourn? What do you do to make to help yourself feel right in the world after someone you've loved has passed away?

We see reminders of her every day. Zahara and Oliver talk about her every day. Mourning is how you think about situations. Sometimes everything reminds me of her, and you get very sad that she went through all of that. I've tried to help Zahara as much as I can with the process and with Oliver. They were closest to her.

Anything else you want to add?

There was Nasrin's pronunciation. Maybe you heard this before, but we would all falling on the floor giggling about how she pronounced certain words. She thought it was really funny too, once we explained what she had said.

I can see her eyes lighting up. She had a good sense of humor.

A really good sense. Yeah, yeah, she made us laugh a lot.

8. Zahara, in person, Nasrin's house, 8-2-2019.

Tell me about yourself.

I grew up in Iliad, New York, and I love it there. I live in Boston with my husband, Adam, and my son, Oliver who I love dearly. I would say I strive to bring love and joy into every situation, a goal in life. I think a lot about who I am and how my Mom was just a beautiful person.

Do you know when your Mom left for the US?

I believe it was 1979? Or maybe 81, 82. She became engaged to my Dad who was here for graduate school (Los Angeles), and she was in Iran, and she wanted to join him but the Revolution started. They ended up getting married over the phone three years later. They divorced when I was one and a half. I was born in 1987 they divorced in 1989, so they were married for seven and a half years.

Did she know much about the US before she came over?

I don't think she did. The US was this idealized place in her mind but she was really excited to move here. There were a lot of things that were very different for her because she had only lived in Iran. Iran was a much more western society before the Revolution. So it was a shock.

Did she have any English before coming over?

She took some in school but really had very little English and that was something she struggled with in the beginning.

Do you know where she first lived in Iliad?

She lived in California, Los Angles, then in Iliad, on Comfort Road renting a basement apartment where I was born. It's a yellow house and the landlord was Martha, but they lived in Sue's house (first), then moved to Comfort Road. After the divorce she rented from Nancy for a few years, then moved back to Sue's.

How long was your mom in Los Angeles?

Around five years. My dad was in a graduate program and then got a post doc at CU and they moved to Iliad. Then my mom became pregnant.

Did she retain any friends from Los Angeles?

I don't think she made too many, she tried, but she didn't speak English well and my Dad he was a bit controlling. She was really lonely. There was one woman she reached out to, maybe five years ago, but no one else.

Did she speak English or Farsi to you?

She always spoke English to me. She said that she was trying to learn English herself, and she was making herself speak English. She tried to teach me Farsi from a book. Words now and then.

Your mother was Muslim. Did you ever go to a mosque?

She was Muslim, and I went to a couple with her in Iran. I never went to one with her here, there weren't any nearby. I think she was raised Muslim and she appreciated that side of herself, she held onto parts of it, and with time she became more spiritual with a belief in God, and she prayed. She was very much accepting of any religion. In Boston she went to Church every week and she had gone to Temple. She was very open to different religions. During the holidays she did celebrate Christmas, she felt like it was a nice tradition for children and she got into it. She loved holidays and celebrated Easter, and the Persian New Year, that was the only Persian holiday she did celebrate. I remember her fasting a few times on Ramadan but it was a thing that she had a tough time with.

Your mom hosted Thanksgiving dinners. Do you remember the first one?

She first did it when I was in elementary school and because she told my Dad, he tried to be nice and he ordered a turkey for us. It was sweet of him but when we got to Wegman's they had already given away the turkey, and there were only pieces – legs, breast, and was like: *oh my gosh, how embarrassing!* She had friends over, and it didn't go as well as she had hoped, but she was an amazing host as you know, and there were so many Thanksgiving dinners after that.

When did your mom buy the house on Hook Place?

I was in third grade, probably eight-years-old, 1996, 97, and she was proud of herself, her first home purchase. The first part of my childhood she had absolutely no money and I have no idea how she made ends meet, and the fact that she was able to buy a house was amazing. I found one of her tax returns from when I was around 3 or 4. She made $1,030.

That's nothing. Did any friends advise her on the house?

I don't remember any of them (Noni, Sue) coming with us to look at houses, I think she mostly figured it out on her own. She liked West Hill because she had friends there. She made a low offer on the first house and it was accepted. We lived there until we sold the house my junior year of high school, so we were there about eight years, then we bought the house on Terrace View.

Your mom would take you periodically back to Iran. Do you remember the first time?

I was five, in kindergarten, and it was the first time she had been back since moving to the US. We went for a month and it was wonderful. She was just so happy to be back with her Mom and sister and brother.

Did she ever have a desire to move back?

No. She saw opportunity for me in the US, that was a big reason, she told me if she didn't have me, she probably would have gone back.

If she had, it would have been easier for my Dad to take custody – if he wanted to – so for my sake and hers we stayed here.

How has your mom's death affected you?

In two ways: the biggest is I was always a very happy person who saw the good in every situation and would find the good. I felt that I was always able to lift myself back up, and I've lost that. I think it will come back, but I feel that I'm in this weird limbo place, numb and floating in life. The other thing is that we were so close, she lived with us the last year and a half of her life, and we talked on the phone sometimes five times a day. I would talk about everything. She was my best friend and I could call her and tell her everything. It's hard not to have that person to talk to. I want to call her when something happens and it's really tough.

And my Mom being sick: I grew from that in a good way: my priorities and how I live my life are completely different now. Before I went to work and worked really hard and wanted to make money and go-go-go. Now, I see so much value in giving as much love as I can to my family. I've become more spiritual so I think I more easily see the good in things (except) that she passed away. There was good that came out of her illness. Hopefully if you talk to me in a year I'll feel there is good coming out of her passing, but I don't feel that yet.

Her passing does it make you think about your own death?

I'm less afraid of death because I thought and read about death when she was sick, and near-death experiences which were moving, full stories, uplifting, but I worry that Oliver will have to go through something like this and I want to do everything I can so he doesn't have to. I'm not worried about dying myself, but I don't want my children to feel this pain and loss at a young age.

How do you mourn?

I'm trying, it's hard, I'm trying to allow myself to feel what I'm feeling. Instead of fighting these emotions, intense emotions sometimes, just allowing myself to have them, my feelings. I try to focus on more of the good memories of her because there were a lot of the horrible ones at the end. The good ones help me. I believe that spirits live on after death. I talk to her and maybe that sounds like a crazy person, but it helps--it makes me feel like I'm still close to her. That's how meditating – it used to help. I tried. Foundation of Light was supportive when my mom was sick and afterward.

8. Yasamin, phone, 2-26- 2020.

Tell me about yourself.

My name is Yasamin and I was born in Baghdad, Iraq, and my mother is Iranian and my father, Iraqi. We moved as immigrants to Canada then the US, then to Iliad in 1994. Iliad is my home. I am a statistician by training and I worked at CU for about 20 years as a founder and director of the Survey Research Institute; for the last five years I've run my own business, Yasamin M. Group, YMG, a data analytic research group.

Do you remember when you first met Nasrin?

Not exactly. There is a group of us in Iliad, my husband affectionately would call us the Middle East Mafia, and we'd get together and Nasrin was amongst them. I can't exactly remember when. It's been a long time.

Did she ever talk to you about Iran?

Yes, because it was very current in her life, and she still has family there, and she used to go back and forth. She did talk about Iran present and Iran past – before she moved to the US.

Did she mention to you why she left Iran?

She got married and came here with her then-husband.

Did you know if she knew much about the country before she left Iran?

Every Middle Easterner knows about the US in some shape or form, you never really know what a place is like until you move and live there. She knew some, but the depth of details and what life would be like for her, no. But none of us do.

Did she mention the struggles she had after she left her husband?

Oh yes, and it was very admirable what she did. She got herself an education that allowed her to have a professional life and income. When she left her husband and she was essentially all alone and she didn't have family here, and she created an incredible life for herself. For an immigrant to come with little resources with a young child, and no support from the father, it was quite impressive what she did, and how much she sacrificed to make an incredible life for her daughter. Yes she did share that, but you've heard that from other people as well.

……..I have. Did she ever express any apprehension about traveling to Iran?

No, she never expressed a concern, not to me. She had her American citizenship.

Do you remember when she got her American citizenship?

No, but she got her citizenship before I did.

Did she ever talk to you about feeling any discrimination or racism because she was Iranian?

That's a loaded question and it implies that people knew her background and unless you ask her, you don't really know. I think she was absolutely loved and respected and admired by anyone who knew her and didn't define her as Iranian. From my perspective, I don't think she actually defined herself that way either, it was a huge part of her heritage and culture and her essence, but it was, I don't think it was a crutch for her. I don't know if you know Iranians in this country are for the most part very accomplished. She's an incredible example of someone who has come with very little in terms of infrastructure, support and means, and through her grit made a successful life for herself and her daughter. That's a testimony to the strength of her Iranian heritage. Iranians are quite impressive in that way. And discriminated because of that? I never heard her say anything to me that she feels that someone was treating her differently because of who she is. She certainly has led a very generous kind life and exposed people who don't know about Iranian culture to the culture by her kindness. If anything she's been a great ambassador for exposing people to the culture.

Has Nasrin impacted your life, and how?

She's impacted my life by being who she is or was, her kindness, her genuineness and I'm sure you've heard this from everyone: her genuine caring for you as her friend, and that's what we have in this life, right? You can trust her unequivocally and she's there without question to help in anyway. She was always available to help, to lend an ear, bring food, go for a walk, whatever. She's quintessentially the essence of kindness, and that's how she impacted my life, a great friend, a lovely friend who just exuded love and kindness. I was very fortunate to have her in my life.

Do you have any kids? Around the same age? Did you connect in that way too?

Her daughter is a little older than my son.

How has her death affected you?

The process of her dying was excruciating, and traumatic and difficult to watch someone you love go through that much pain. To watch her daughter go through it, that was jarring and painful. And to lose her, it's a huge loss, the loss of a very dear friend. You have friendships that are cultivated over time you grow together. When you lose someone that dear and that special that leaves a hole in your life and your heart. Hopefully over time what she has left us is her legacy of kindness, that I hope to continue emulating. Obviously no one can be Nasrin, but trying to emulate her kindness and pass it forward to others. She has left me with this indelible mark of human kindness, and how much one person who's not necessarily extremely wealthy or the most intelligent person on the planet or the most successful, what she had is beyond all that, and much more valuable. What I've learned and what I want to do to is keep her legacy alive and emulate her as much as I possibly can. She was exceptional. But if all of us can think a little bit about Nasrin and carry her with us, since she's touched other people's lives, I think she'd be very happy with us all. I want to continue remembering her goodness of her, not her suffering.

Several people have said that going through the process of her illness, and death has made them more spiritual. Do you want to comment?

Whenever you lose someone dear and precious to you it forces you to look at your own life and reflect about what's important, and what can we learn from this, what can we take away. It does force you to reevaluate your priorities, or at least reconfirm your priorities. For me spirituality is unique to each individual, it's important to them, and however or whatever gives them comfort in this life. It certainly forces you, as you lose these precious people in your life, to think: *Am I doing the best I possibly can with the time I have on this planet with the people most important to me?* Have I become more spiritual? I'm not sure it's impacted me that way. Do I feel there are things in this life that are out of my control that need a higher power or something? Absolutely. There's that that I don't understand about this life and this world, but it certainly does remind you in a very dramatic way: *why am I here? Where are my priorities? What is meaningful to me?* That certainly has been the impact of losing that sweet woman. And again, another reminder: how do we want to treat other people? I think that I was probably more tough, more demanding, and now it allows me to look at people very differently: kinder, gentler, and not so hard. And how I want to impact people: I want to be more kind, more thoughtful.

Has Nasrin's death made you think about your own death?

Not so much, and I don't know if you know, I lost my husband in August.

I'm sorry.

Certainly death is traveling too close to me. I think it's going to be our reality, I don't dwell on it, it's going to come, whenever it comes, but again as I said, I just want to focus more on what impact I can make while I'm here, eventually I won't be here, so while I am here, I'm not going to spend my time thinking about the inevitable which I can't control and losing people so close to you is painful, and difficult and leaves a gap in your heart and your soul. I'm trying to reconcile it with: what is my main purpose in life? Am I leading my life as Nasrin and my husband did? These are people who really made a difference. That's how I look at it, but not my own death, not so much.

……..Before I started interviewing people, I did not understand that people grieve differently. How do you grieve?

I'm not sure how to answer that. Sadness, crying and an intense sense of loneliness. And just trying to find resources, to understand, trying to figure out how not to be alone. That's a difficult question, because I don't know. I'm going through it, but I don't know what I'm going through: the feelings of it, the mechanics of it, reading and trying to find solace and being with people that I love.

Is there anything else you want to say about Nasrin?

Just that she was certainly one of those people that we were all very lucky to have in our lives, and the joy and love she spread from being herself was huge. She is missed and that legacy she leaves us all is that legacy of kindness. Although she had challenges in her life, she produced beauties in her wake. Her daughter and her grandchild are her biggest legacy. Her daughter is an incredible woman and she did that so well, and that's a huge gift she's given to the world.

As I said we're all here just a short time and we need to figure out how to leave this world a little bit better from what was handed to us. Certainly Nasrin did that. That was a gift to us all.

10. Julia and Shiv, phone, 11-2-2019.

Tell me about yourself.

My husband and I are physicians and we work in the hospital. Nasrin is my mother's cousin, and she and my mother are like sisters. Nasrin was like an aunt.

Do you remember when you met Nasrin?

I had known her my whole life and had spoken to her as a child, but I lived in Sweden and didn't meet her until three or four years ago when we travelled to the US. It was in Boston, in January 2017, when I was going to a course. I reached out to Zahara and met Adam too.

What is your impression of Nasrin, if you were going to describe her.

Very warm and definitively welcoming, she put people at ease. Very caring, sweet and kind, asking, 'Are you okay?' My husband met her about six months ago when she flew to our wedding; a week before the wedding, in the UK, in London, subsequently we had the opportunity to come back with them to the US and we stayed with Zahara in Boston.

Did she ever talk to you about Iran?

Not a huge amount. I know I have lots of extended family there: my mum's and her family, they all grew up there, I don't know much in terms of details. I've never been to Iran myself.

Why?

I have never been because my parents left during the Islamic Revolution. My dad had been very vocal and still is vocal against the regime. I have his surname and he could never go back. It's overcautious and I worry – you never know what the regime would do with people who were vocal. I would love to go, just not with the current government.

Has Nasrin's death changed you in any way?

I never had a relative or friend be seriously ill before partly because I don't have all of my family – they're in Iran and partly this has not happened yet. She's the first relative. I see a lot of people die and be very ill at work, but this is the first person I knew personally and I think this does give you a different perspective on death. With her particularly it opened my mind to the importance of life. My husband and I are oncologists and we spoke to her about whether she should be pursuing more aggressive chemo, and I know she was very adamant, she wanted to pursue alternative therapy. We initially disagreed: *This is not a wise choice at the time.* She ended up having a really good year of life, she was very happy – she had hope, you think back and what gives you hope. Had she been on the chemotherapy to extend her life – two months – is it worth it if means vomiting and feeling not so well? Her experience definitely changed my views around death and palliative care and things like that, and just the vulnerability of life because she's the first person I had affection for who died. You don't take health for granted with family and friends.

How old are you?

Twenty-eight. My husband is older. He's thirty-six.

Has this experience – Nasrin's end stage of life – has it made you feel more spiritual?

Personally – no, to be very honest. And part of that is having grown up in Sweden, which is an atheist country. I can completely appreciate that especially if you're spiritual as a child but this has never been a part of my life.

How do you mourn? How do you reconcile her death and life?

Initially, driving home after I heard, the first time, I cried. Then after a while, after the initial shock, we just felt upset. I think I'm desensitized – I see a lot of death generally, I'm quite desensitized and I'm a pragmatist. I think: *I'm going to let this remind me of how precious life is and not take life for granted.* I guess it's to remind me to appreciate the good things. I feel upset not just because Nasrin passed away but I know it had a big effect on my mother. Nasrin was probably the closest family member to my mother. I get upset about what my mother lost because she lost someone who was very close to her.

Is there anything else you or Shiv want to add?

I (Shiv) first knew her from over the phone. She spoke to me about her cancer and essentially – I'm an oncologist too – I gave her my opinion which she disagreed with me. And to tell the truth, I'll be honest, it completely changed the way I thought about a lot of it, because you do what you think is in her best interest, but she didn't want to go ahead with the chemo, and actually the condition she had was terminal. She declined, and that surprised me. She gave me a reason: she wouldn't be able to do what she wanted, she actually wanted to come to our wedding the year before she died. And up until the last few weeks she actually had a good quality of life. She was very happy to travel. The flight to London which is quite a long journey, and then she was engaged in all aspects of our wedding and that taught me something. I have to say she's always been someone who was warm and friendly and very outgoing. My parents met her for that week and liked her as well. Even though she was in a room of 30 or 40 people she was one of the biggest personalities. She directed the conversation and was very interested in people as well. And very sweet – one of her nice qualities.

She had lots of friends from diverse backgrounds.

She really liked people. Yes.

11. Marie, in person, 10-11-19.

Tell me a little about yourself.

I have two jobs – I am a consultant for non-profits – mostly spiritual retreat centers – and I am a holistic healer.

Have you always lived in Iliad?

I was born in Spain but brought up all over the world. I came to college here and moved away, and like a lot of people, moved back years later. When looking to settle down we did a tour of the northeast and, after visiting a lot of places, we realized what a unique gem Iliad was. We came back in 2003, bought this house in 2004, then left again to run another spiritual retreat center for seven years. We've been back and forth several times, but Iliad feels like home. It's a special place, as you know.

Do you remember the first time you met Nasrin?

I don't, but I know I met her walking her dog Hershey on the bike trail. For years we would pass each other there and let our dogs greet each other – in fact we knew the dogs' names before we knew each other's! She always had a bright smile that seemed genuine, and we just had a certain kind of ease, a recognition of each other somehow. We'd see each other and share tidbits of our lives, but nothing too serious until she became ill.

Did Nasrin ever tell you about her past life in Iran?

I do past life regressions (laugh), but I don't think that's what you're asking about. Yes she did, she told me about growing up there and about her family.

Did she tell you why she came to the US?

She got married and came with her husband, but I don't remember too many details. I will say – in full disclosure – that I saw her as a client, so there are things that came up, excavating her childhood for instance, that I'm not at liberty to share.

Has Nasrin's death affected you?

Yes. I'm not sure if knowing someone so intimately can not affect you. It's interesting: up until the last couple of years, I had never really experienced much death. Then in the span of a year and a half there were several deaths, all right in a row. The biggest effect for me was that it hammered home in a palpable way the preciousness of life and the temporary nature of this existence. Obviously we know that cerebrally, but it's strange and unsettling to see a person regularly and then suddenly they are no longer there. In Nasrin's case, I was there as she passed, and as I knelt by her body on the bed, I could actually feel her being, her presence still there, but unattached to her body. I've experienced this with animals but it was the first time that I experienced this with a person. What I know is that life continues on, and I know this sounds like a cliché, but we are never separate after being connected with someone.

What was remarkable about Nasrin, through her illness and pain, even when hanging on by a thread, she would ask me, *How are you doing?* One of the last things she said to me in the last days was that she wanted to cook for me! Up to the end, she was always thinking of others. And when she asked *How are you?* she had a way of looking at you deeply in the eyes, unhurried and sincerely wanting to connect at a deeper heart level. She lived and she shone so exceptionally in that way, it was clear that she was tapped into something more. Her genuine kindness and generous heart continue to inspire me.

Feeling her presence did that go on for a long time? Minutes?

Much longer than that, she was there that evening, the whole time I was there, and I assume beyond that. I had close contact with her for days. She was still around for the funeral and for a while after. She wanted to stay close to watch over Zahara and her grandson (well, to everybody, but particularly Zahara). I connected with her from time to time in my meditations, and finally there came a time where she was wondering if staying close was a benefit to Zahara, or if it was preventing Zahara from moving into the next phase of her transition. Even on the other side, she was most concerned about others.

Do you still feel her presence?

I tune into her from time and time, and there are random times when she pops in.

Has Nasrin's death made you think about your own death more?

Not more, but I would say I am a person who probably thinks about my own death a lot more than the average person. I don't find it morbid at all. Thinking about death helps us live more intentionally, more fully. I don't have a fear of death. I know that we go on.

How do you mourn?

For me, I just let the feelings flow freely, when and how they come. The trickiest part about leading her funeral was that I had to hold it together. I knew if I let my feelings run free, I'd be blubbering and be unable to speak. I visited the gravesite the evening prior, and let some tears out then. Just after the funeral, I let the tears flow and let my body shake and sob. Otherwise, I feel the sadness, the absence, the impact she had on my life, I recall memories and relive them in my mind. Mostly when I think of her my heart smiles, even while I feel her absence.

Is there anything else you want to say about Nasrin?

She was an extraordinary individual. She's in my personal Hall of Fame of people I've known who have impacted me and shaped my life for the better. Her authentic kindness and thoughtfulness will stay with me forever. She always seemed to live so selflessly and generously, with a generous heart, despite her personal circumstances. As I learned more of her life, what she went through and overcame, I saw that there was a quiet determined powerhouse in that sweet beautiful package. It was inspiring to witness her compassion, even when she shared about difficult situations or people that hurt or frustrated her, she didn't have a mean word to say about them. She'd let it go, set boundaries, find a way, move on, but she never had a need to diminish others. She left me with a lasting example of the power of pure presence – when you were with her she was completely with you. One of my favorite pictures is of her in a beautiful dress, elegant as usual, on the floor playing with her grandson, oblivious to everything else, to everyone else, completely and wholeheartedly present in love. May I be more like that!

12. Alice, in person, 2-2-2020.

Tell me about yourself.

I'm 62, and I grew up in Iliad, and I moved away and went to music school. Music and singing are my passion. I had a small job as a French teacher. I was mostly a stay-at-home mom with four children, ages 22 to 32. I love being active, moving and swimming. My husband and I are building a house in Ellis Hollow where I grew up. There was a cabin and we've made it into a more livable house. It's insulated and there's heat and water, things like that.

Do you remember the first time you met Nasrin?

Yes. Definitely at Noni's house. Nasrin was living there, maybe? Or renting Kumi's (Noni's Mom) apartment. Then Hannah was Zahara's age, and they became friends, along with Maia (Noni's daughter), who was a year younger. I just remember the three of them, little children playing and just how sweet that was. Nasrin was never anything but sweet, just loving and sweet. Most of the time I saw her in connection with Noni.

What were the conversations like that you had with her?

I'm remembering the more recent conversations, how she would always ask about me, my children, how I was, and Dana, and she hardly ever talked about herself. If I asked about her, she'd say, *I'm okay. I'm fine.* You know she didn't ever go into great detail but she was always so interested, so caring about what was going on in my life, and my children's lives.

Did she ever talk about Iran?

Close to her death, she did talk about Iran, but they were sensory memories, how things smelled, the look of beauty of the country. She didn't talk too much about anything political. As you're asking me this I'm regretting that I didn't find out more about the family.

Anything else you want to say about Nasrin?

She was beautiful through and through. I'm saying that emphatically. Her eyes, you know, and Zahara has those eyes too. Nasrin was kind, and she had this immense beauty and grace and generosity and when I hear about how she struggled, and then to see someone so generous, who didn't have much to give in terms of her monetary situation, but she gave all her heart. And in cooking--she was an amazing cook. You'd go to her house and she'd have these spreads. Zahara and Hannah became good friends in high school so there were more occasions where we would see each other. Whenever the kids were in town, she would always make these beautiful spreads.

Did she ever talk much about her early life in Iliad?

Actually I found about a lot of that at the memorial service.

Has Nasrin's passing changed you in any way?

Yes. I would go visit a few times when she was dying. She kept saying to me that my presence – she liked me being there with her. She made me appreciate that one's presence is enough; not just my presence, but anyone's. There's something palpable about it. Her heart was right there. It was poignant for me to understand that you don't have to do anything in particular. I always feel bad I didn't cook something or I didn't do something, but just showing up and being there was appreciated. As humans, we show that our hearts are a quiet presence. Our essence. That's a lot. Nasrin gave me that. I did not know her that well, but her presence, yes, it's still palpable. I miss her even though I didn't know hang out with her that much.

Have you had other family or friends die?

I lost my dad when I was little. My mom died when I was 34, my sister when I was 36. And I had a dear friend whose husband died while hiking this past August.

How did you mourn them? How do you mourn?

I think initially it's so important to have some kind of memorial. I know there are people that don't do that, because they feel like it's egocentric. I am so grateful when there is a memorial service. Nasrin's was beautiful. It was such a key piece of that mourning. When my dad died, I didn't think about it, back in those days people wouldn't talk about death. It's so important. My friend whose husband died this summer is amazing: she's keeping it conscious and reaching out to her friends and she's talking about it. That that's important, as painful as it is. It gets more painful if you don't. I don't know what Zahara is doing about it. I hope and I think she is. It's important to keep remembering and talking about it. She sends us those beautiful memories and photographs. Not being afraid of crying, or being with my friend when she's in tears. She's very quick to just burst into tears, and my god, you can get nervous: what do I do with this person is in tears in front of me? Do I pretend that nothing's happening or just sit with it? That's an important question.

Has Nasrin's passing changed you?

The fact that you're gone from this realm makes life more precious. When someone has touched you as Nasrin did, I feel emotion rising. A piece of her is ingrained in me. You remember deeply her eyes, her kindness, her courage. Incredible sweetness and grace. Hopefully some of this rubbed off on me. And to persevere like she did in the midst of pain.

Hannah mentioned that she's spiritual, and she said that you're spiritual, and I was wondering: did you discuss spirituality in any way with Nasrin?

Definitely. Not so much in a religious way, because I didn't grow up with any particular religion, but I was interested in Eastern religions, meditation, Buddhist practices and yoga. Nasrin was interested in that. A few times I sent her chants. I don't know what her religious background was, I think she was more interested in spirituality.

Meditation. Especially in the last weeks when I visited her at her house and she was really frail. She liked talking about those kinds of things. I liked being peaceful around her and she appreciated it.

Anything else you want to add?

She was an amazing woman. What a beautiful mom with all the love and support. Zahara flourished. Just a sweetheart. I see that Nasrin lives in Zahara, very strongly.

13. Zahara, Nasrin's house, 10-29-2019.

How are you doing?

How am I doing, like with my mom?

Yes, or in general.

In terms of losing her, I'm doing better than I was before, there's still difficult times, but they come less frequently. We're trying to move forward with life. We have Oliver and a baby on the way which just gives you hope and joy.

What else have you been up to?

We're planning to move to Iliad. We've been trying to clean out both this house and the house in Boston. I've been staying home with Oliver, so I do a lot of kid things during the week. Fun kid activities.

I remember those days. In terms of mourning your mom's passing, how are you?

I feel more like myself these days which is good; for a while it didn't feel like my mind was functioning as it normally does. I can now meditate and it helps, but there's still challenges that I'm working through. Obviously difficult moments and, trying to get used to everything. It's a process.

You're a life coach. Do you feel these challenges you've had could be helpful in some way?

I'm hoping it will help me with other people. I am facing challenges that I hadn't faced before and working through them.

Last time we talked you mentioned your mom lived in Los Angeles. You wouldn't happen to have any of her Los Angeles contacts, would you?

No. There was one woman that she was friends with that she had connected with 10 years ago. Just one phone call. They became Facebook friends. The only person who would know would be my dad, and he's not the best person to contact about this. I don't know that she had many friends there. When she was married, she was very isolated.

Did she talk much about that time in her life?

Every once in a while. She tried to avoid putting my dad down because she always thought, he's my father and she wants us to have a good relationship, but I do know he was controlling, and she felt isolated. He put her down and it was not a good time of her life.

You mentioned going to Iran when you were five years old. 1992. You went for a month. Did your mom have any hesitation about going back?

At that time I don't think she did. The relationship between the US and Iran was good at that point and she wanted to see her family. Before that the relationship was pretty bad and so she waited. And financially – tickets were expensive.

Was it difficult getting in Iran?

Not really. We both have Iranian passports. And my mother spoke Farsi. That made it that made it easier.

And what about coming back to the US?

I don't think it was that challenging, sometimes they asked you a lot of questions, for instance, *what was the purpose of the trip?* But the fact is we have dual citizenship. I don't think she actually had an American citizenship at that point. I do remember once, when we were either going or coming back to the airport in Iran, they stole my birth certificate. They asked to see it and then they wouldn't give it back to my mom. We never got the original back.

Interesting.

Often they'll have you bribe them to let you through, but I think that happens to almost everybody.

When you were in Iran, did you feel restricted? For instance, did you need a head scarf to walk outside?

Once you are over nine-years-old, as a female, you have to be covered. It's a little thing and for someone not used to it, it's not very pleasant. Women have to be covered from head to toe. You never know when you're walking down the street, if you're going to get stopped by a police officer. They may ask you questions and so you definitely don't feel as safe, or as comfortable and free as you do here. Other than that, you do have freedom to walk around and go wherever you want, but you have to abide by their rules.

Would you would you have felt comfortable walking the streets by yourself?

I don't think so. I don't speak the language well and I don't know the culture well and if I had been stopped by a police officer I don't think I would have been able to handle it in the right way. They can be really unpredictable. They can arrest you for no reason at all and hold you as long as they want. That would have scared me.

It seems to me that your mom was very courageous to go back to Iran.

Yes, it was a different culture there than when she left, but her family meant the world to her. And she grew up there.

Did you go out at night when you were in Iran?

Not walking, but it's really common to like go to friends' houses at night, usually by car. So you get in your car and then drive there, and then drive back so you don't actually have to be out and about.

Is there anything that you remember about Iran that struck you?

The warmth of the people. They're all very, very open with their emotions and in a kind and loving and generous way that makes you feel welcome. My mom brought that with her, and those qualities made her stand out in this culture, because it's not something that people (here) are as open with. It's also a more lively culture: there's lots of music and dancing and get-togethers. People are always coming to each other's houses. There's more family and community closeness than here.

What was the name of the city where your mom grew up?
Amol.

That's right. Was it a big city?

It's definitely bigger than Iliad, but not huge. I'm not sure what the population is if I had to guess I would say maybe a few hundred thousand.

And it was near the sea?

It's about an hour from the Caspian Sea. It's pretty easy to get there.

Did you ever go to Tehran?

We would fly when we went there, but we didn't spend too much time there. It's certainly a much bigger, and more westernized city.

How many times did you go back to Iran?

In kindergarten, and I think after seventh grade. Maybe once before. Once in college and then once after, so five times.

Did your mom go every year?

She went those five times with me and then I think she went two more times without me.

Did she ever express any reservations about going back? Were there times when the relationship between the US and Iran were not so good that might have stopped her from going back?

The only time that it concerned her was when she first moved here: she planned to go back every year but relations were so bad that she didn't. Then the last few years since Trump has been president, but she went back recently. She suggested, because I wanted to take Adam and Oliver with me, waiting to take them because they're not Iranian citizens. I know American citizens have been detained.

I finished reading a book on Iran, hoping to understand how our relationship got to the point that it's at now. It's sad. Americans used to go to Iran and now that doesn't happen. When you were in Iran and among your relatives and friends, were you able to talk about the political situation, or was it too dangerous?

In person you can talk about it. When you're talking on the phone the phone will often cut out if you start talking about politics. Or, if you try to type anything I think they monitor that as well. So I would say people openly talk about it in person but not in any way that could be monitored.

I had read that the largest Iranian population in the United States is in Los Angeles. Do you know if there are other Iranian population centers?

I'm not sure. I've heard that there's community in the Long Island area, I know there's some outside Boston. They're smaller. The biggest community is in Los Angeles.

Do you know the size of the Iranian community in Iliad?

There's not a ton of people. There is an Iranian student organization at CU that puts on events that Persians from the community attend. Other than that, there's a handful of Persian families, and a lot of them know each other, like my mother knew Zhila.

So right now, students from Iran are studying here in the US?

Yes. It's probably more difficult to come to the US but there are events here so there must be people. There was also a Persian class at CU.

Interesting. Have you gone to any of those events or are you planning to?

I went to a couple and I took the Persian classes when I was at CU. My mom would often take her family to them because she thought that it would make them feel more comfortable here.

……..Nasrin's family members who are coming over now, is it dangerous for them to come over and go back? Do you have a sense of that?

It doesn't seem like it's been dangerous, I haven't really seen that. My one cousin here just became a US citizen, not M. , his sister, Maril. She was going to go back, but she's worried now that she's a US citizen that they might give her a hard time, so she's decided to wait. But the rest have green cards so it's not a problem.

Do you follow the news in Iran?

Not as well as I should. It's something big happens I usually hear about it.

Do you have any desire to go back?

I would love to go back. There are people in my family who I won't see if I don't go back: my grandmother, and some of my dad's relatives. I also want Oliver and Adam to experience that culture because it is so different. The question about what strikes me about that culture-- just coming to mind is that in certain areas of Iran, the lifestyle is very old fashioned, in a sweet way: there are sheepherders and other people who live in the mountains. They're disconnected from anything westernized.

But it would be strange to go back without my mom because she was the link to everybody in the family. I don't speak the language that well. Hopefully at some point, I will be able to.

How is Persian different from Farsi? Is it a different language?

It's the same language; for some reason, people interchange the two words. Everybody in Iran speaks Farsi and then everybody also has the dialect of their state. My mom's state was Mazandaran, and she spoke Mazandarani and Farsi.

Farsi is the national language.

Yes.

But there are dialects, so if you lived in one part of Iran, you might speak a totally different language from another part?

Yes, there are very different languages.

And I've been reading that citizens, there are either referred to as Iranians, or Persians. Is there a difference?

I think technically they would be Iranians but a lot of them, myself included, refer to them as Persians just because it used to be part of the Persian Empire.

What do Iranians think of Americans?

They generally like Americans. Politics is often really different from your actual day-to-day cultural interactions between people. Iranians generally like the culture. Products from the US are highly regarded; for instance, if you brought clothes, makeup or any sort of American product they would be really excited, but they're always excited when people come here. Iranians are very welcoming with people who aren't Persian.

Television in Iran: are the programs Iranian or American?

They're mostly Iranian, I'm pretty sure, but you might be able to find American programs.

The reason I ask is because there's such a paucity, a sparseness of information that we get here from Iran, and so I'm wondering how, if you were in Iran, how you would know what it's like, what Americans are like, unless you met an American?

They still hear about pop culture in the US but that might skew their vision of Americans and women. They might think that everybody lives glamorous lives. That's often something that that I've heard from people that have moved here, that they thought life would be so glamorous and easy, and then they realize like they actually have to work really hard. Life isn't like what you see on TV. Interacting with Americans doesn't happen so often.

So there might be censorship in terms of American TV programs but not music. Or, is it possible for them to go on the internet, for instance, I don't know what the internet is like there, but can you Google search, for instance, The Beatles?

My cousins who live in Iran know a lot about the music in the US, so there must be a way that they're getting it. There is censorship so my guess is that they're probably ways around it, but I'm not sure what they are.

We were talking about how Nasrin had many diverse friends.

I can think of 10 people who she'd call family.

In talking with the friends of your mom's, I've seen sides of your mom that I didn't that I didn't know existed.

Each time, if you look at her friends, it's not like she had a stereotypical type of friend. Each one has their own distinct personality and brought something different to the table. She had a different relationship with each of them, but still genuine and close.

Exactly. She was intimate with all of us.

She really had this amazing ability to read people so well, and understand them deeply, that she could connect with many diverse people, she could see what was dear and important to a friend and connect with them on that level. It could be something completely different for one person versus another. But she still somehow made strong connections.

And she also was never afraid to take a risk.

I think about what she went through especially when I was younger. She was so courageous, even just staying here in the United States. Putting herself through school. I'm not sure if I told you this last time but I always just loved the story of when she decided that she wanted to go to X ray school, because she wanted a better life than what babysitting was providing.

You didn't tell me.

So she decided she wanted to go.

Did somebody advise her?

I'm guessing that she probably talked to Sue about it just because they were very close and Sue's husband worked at the hospital. I never asked her that. But she knew that the person who got the highest grades in the class would get a full scholarship so she applied and was not accepted. When she didn't get in, she found out where the admissions officer lived, the head of the program. She went to his house and knocked on the door, and introduced herself and said: *This is so important for me. I really want a better life for my daughter and I promise you if you let me in, I'll get the highest grade in the class, and I will be your best student.* And he said: *We're full this year but you're in for next year.* Then she lived up to that promise. She barely spoke English and was working and going to school and she somehow did really well and got a full scholarship.

To have that kind of courage –to go to somebody's house and knock on the door and say what she said. I don't know anyone else would have done that.

She had this little cuteness about her that made it, the way that she went about things, it was adorable and sweet.

And she was humble.

Very humble.

14. Sorayya K., in person, 8-31-19

Tell me about yourself.

I have been living in Iliad since 1996 and I have two sons, Kamal, who is 27 and Shahid who is 23, and I moved to Iliad in 1996 and that's when I met you. Prior to that I'm from Pakistan, my mother is Dutch and my father was Pakistani. I was born in Vienna and grew up in Islamabad and came here when I was 17 to Pennsylvania to a small college called Allegheny College. I went to graduate school at the University of Denver which is where I met Naeem, my husband. He teaches at Iliad College. After we left Denver we moved to Syracuse and we were there for seven or eight years where both boys were born, and we moved to Iliad. And I am a writer, by the way!

Do you remember the first time you met Nasrin?

I do not. I have been thinking about that especially in preparation for the Memorial service, I must have met her first at your house, probably at one of your Red House parties; I'm confused because I remember Zahara when she was in high school, so I feel like I knew her for a long time. I became close to Nasrin after my mother was diagnosed with cancer but prior to that I remember my sister was visiting and we all went to Nasrin's for dinner, and she spent Thanksgiving with us once. That was when Zahara was dating an Iranian. Nasrin didn't like him. Steve? I feel like she joined us for a couple of desserts, she participated in celebrations at our home.

I recall that we were at some event at your house, Christmas one year because my mother was there, and I remember Anna telling my mother that she had interviewed Nasrin for some project. Another time much later – my mother was diagnosed in 2012, I asked Nasrin, *how are you doing?* She asked about the boys and told me that her father died of leukemia maybe when she was 13. She's the eldest? He died around Eid – a Muslim holiday – and I was struck because she didn't like to celebrate Eid as a result. Nasrin and her siblings did not know that their father was dying or diagnosed. Maybe the kids didn't find out until later. I was thinking about this in terms of my mother.

Did Nasrin ever tell you why she left Iran?

I heard about Nasrin's story from you but I also had one really long conversation after Nasrin was diagnosed, maybe after Zahara got married. We walked to East Hill and had coffee at CTB and she told me her life story which I wish I had taped. She left Iran because she was married to someone who had American citizenship. My understanding is she married over the phone – this guy either had a green card or already had citizenship. That was my memory. I didn't know much about her life prior to that. At the Memorial service there was this beautiful photo at the Foundation for Life, Nasrin in a wedding dress with her mother. When I saw that I recalled the story. Nasrin told me how things had gone badly between her and her husband. I want to say he was abusive towards her. She told me when Zahara was small, she'd already left. He turned her into immigration, prior to her having a green card. INS, or the police, came to her house in the middle of the night, Zahara was small and she begged them to allow her to show up at the police station or wherever in the morning she had to go. Somehow that was arranged and she was told by a lawyer or friend that it would be almost impossible to get residency given her situation. There was this one chance: if she could show a judge (I don't know if this was specifically for Iranians) that she was doing everything to better herself, and provide for her livelihood for herself and the child, that the judge would have power to be lenient. She stood before the judge and explained all that she was doing: working (two jobs?), going to school, maybe babysitting and looking after Zahara. The judge took leniency on her and granted her working papers or a green card. She impressed upon me how unusual it was for anyone to succeed in this circumstance and that was kind of miraculous. She was forthcoming in that conversation, how difficult it had been, how meaningful and fulfilling to be Zahara's mother. To have succeeded in a career, and to have taken care of herself – we shared something – obviously being Muslim and this idea of succeeding on your own without a family, I appreciate that, and was amazed by her strength and preservation.

Anything else you want to add about Nasrin?

Nasrin and I started to become close when my mother was diagnosed in 2012, she passed in June 2016, and I feel this conversation happened in July. After my mother passed, Nasrin came to the house to offer condolences and we were sitting on the deck, and I gave her coffee. She gave me an orchid and she cried with me, literally we cried on the deck about my mother's passing, gosh, she was so full of love and care, and Naeem came out and sat with us, he had tears in his eyes. This was after Nasrin had been diagnosed. I felt my mortality. All the worries that come along with that diagnosis were there in her heart, I think she was already imagining Zahara's loss which for those of us have lost parents we have some comprehension of how large the void is. That was quite an amazing interaction at that time. Nasrin introduced me to meditation shortly thereafter (fall 2016), that's when I started to join her and in that conversation after my mother passed – I have sleep issues. I was telling her I how I couldn't sleep and couldn't focus or read or work so she said: why don't you come to meditation? Honestly, I thought little of it, I made fun of it, but I was at such a loss I thought: why not go? It would be fun to do. We went and that's when I met Sevag and Menache. We all started to go to meditation and Nasrin was a pillar of support to me during that time. It's kind of amazing she has so much love for so many people in so many different ways. She had a lot of close friends and cultivated so many different kinds of people. It's an unusual person to bring that all together. Just look at the people at her memorial service, so many different kinds. People would say, *I didn't know you knew Nasrin!* She leaves behind that community of love and strength and joy – joy for life and beauty. I remember how she'd say with a twinkle in her eye: *You know what I'm saying?* Right?

Yes. Did she ever talk to you about returning to Iran?

Permanently? No. I know she loved going back to visit, I never heard her say she wanted to stay. But we did talk about how important it was to stay in touch with her mother and to visit. I know that she visited her Mom last August and I remember when she told me she was going, she was resplendent, beaming to say she was able to go. That's when she had been on the raw food diet, but mostly living in Boston with Zahara. I regret not catching up with her right after that so I could hear more about the journey. I did talk to her briefly and I know that it went well. She mentioned some stuff about her family, her mother was living with Nasrin's brother and his wife in the family home. Nasrin's mother didn't much care for the daughter- in- law, she made things difficult for her, and eventually the brother asked the mother to leave, and the mother did leave. She bought an apartment and was living by herself when Nasrin visited. Nasrin was worried but her mother said: *Listen, I love it. I'm away from the daughter-in-law. I wasn't very comfortable there.* She was more comfortable on her own and enjoyed that visit with Nasrin. She went to see her brother and they made a plan to meet – but not in the family house (Nasrin didn't want to go there). At the last minute her brother co-opted her and they did visit at the old house. Nasrin was not happy.

I was always interested in Iran, what it looked like to her and in my imagination as well and growing up in Pakistan at the time when Iran and Pakistan were turbulent politically. What did the mountains look like? I had done some research for one of my novels about that and sometimes I would ask her. They had a summer home in the mountains, I can't remember specifically where it was. I remember they did not tell her mother about her illness although her mother kept asking, as if she intuited there was something wrong. Everyone would say she had hurt her shoulder and was unwell because of that, moving slowly. That hindered her. I know she was so happy to go back. I don't think she thought she was going to say goodbye to everyone – she was or had been going through chemo. She wasn't sure she would have an opportunity to go back. It meant a lot to her.

Has Nasrin's death, has it made you think more about your own death?

Sort of, not that I have a preoccupation with death, but it adds to the register of grief as deaths do. It makes me think so much about Zahara because I felt such a loss when my mother died, and I was not as close to my mother as Nasrin and Zahara were, but I feel such emptiness and it's difficult to come to terms with it. I feel like I'm still dragging and it makes me think as a grown adult with two kids, not much older than Zahara, about their potential loss, losing me or Naeem. There's a poem about a poet trying to imagine the loss for her children when she passes. She's worried about it.

Mother's Prayer by Athena Kildegarrd

Stood on the porch of our raised cottage
and saw my two ruddy children
crouched below in the grass
over a hard-backed beetle
and I was taken with this phobia
that goes up and up with me
and suddenly I saw myself fallen
my body twisted on the pavement
a thigh bare and scraped and bloody
with my two children, wooden
with fear, bent over me
saying softly, "mama, mama."

And I knew then as one comes to know
things that lodge themselves in us
that I had no way of telling them
my children, how I would
leave them some day as ashes
they will toss out over moving water,
how they will feel abandoned
in ways that even dreams cannot express
lord, make room inside me for this.

Nasrin's grave is close to my house and I walk about every day so I do visit her grave. I feel that visiting is paying respect to her and giving. I recite a Muslim prayer at her grave, a short verse I repeat three times. Every time I go, I feel the earth has swallowed her up more. The grass is growing over it and there's less and less an imprint of her. Somehow she still feels alive, not just in Zahara but in daily events. Sometimes when I wake up in the morning and see the sun rising, I think if Nasrin could see the colors she would be astonished. Moments like that I think about her, just as I think about my parents at different times of the day. I feel like Nasrin was very brave in the face of death and my mother was as well, she was more concerned about us then she was about her pain, her misery, because in the end it was misery.

How do you mourn?

Maybe walking to Nasrin's grave, which is a way of paying respect although sometimes when I stand there, I feel a closeness to Nasrin, I almost hear her laughing. It feels it's important to respect her memory. Naeem has come once or twice and it's not only respecting the dead but also a way of confronting what's going to happen to all of us. It's important for us to do that. I try to go once or twice a week. It's a ritual. I also think we mourn by absorbing loss – you have more respect for the beauty and joy and love in life. Remembering Nasrin on a beautiful day when I go to Steward Park is also a way of mourning. It's a more hopeful way.

> Poem read at Nasrin's Service
>
> Even
>
> All this time
> The sun never says to the earth,
> "You owe
> Me."
> Look
> What happens
> With a love like that,
> It lights the
> Whole
> Sky.
>
> -Hafiz

15. Zhila, in person, 7-13-2019.

Tell me about yourself.

I left for Los Angeles to get a Master's in Public Administration when I was 23 or 24, a few months after the Revolution. All of my family eventually came here. I married my husband, who is Iranian, in Madison, Wisconsin, where he got a faculty position. Then he got a position at CU, and we moved to Iliad. I got a degree in accounting and have been working in *Grants and Contracts* for CU's Lab of O for 25 years. I was at home for 10 years to bring up my sons, Miyad and Ata. That was when I got the degree in accounting.

What brought you to the US?

I got a bachelors' degree from the American University in Iran and planned to get a Master's here because I was accepted to Southern California. You never know what's going to happen in your country and it's surprising that it did take. Things got worse, and then the war. We all believed that the Khomeini rule would be temporary. Because of the potential for war and conscription, my niece and nephew were brought over. Eventually everyone started to come over. Iran was not a good place to go back to. They really didn't have any other choices. They were at the American School and it's not always easy to make it in a new country. We worked hard to get our degrees and jobs, and permanent residence, and it was not easy. Meanwhile the political situation in Iran did not get any better: people were living normal lives but the political situation – it affected your life. My parents were affected. They sacrificed and sent money through the black market to ensure opportunities for their children and grandchildren. We finished our degrees. Our parents didn't want to come but eventually emigrated because they were lonely, and my father lost the strength of getting on a plane – the long travel. They stayed with my brother in Los Angeles. They sold everything back in Iran and brought the money here. Now it is more difficult to bring money here. We knew we didn't want to go back: when you're not in a country for 35 years and there is a revolution, it is difficult. The regulations and laws for businesses have changed. We had to start from scratch, but now I am more at home here. It was good for our kids.

Have you been back to Iran?

The older boy went to Iran when he was eight for two months, but they never had the chance again: you're always concerned that if they go, because there is no American Embassy, and you are Iranian by the mother's blood, no matter what, their mother is Iranian and anything could happen to him. He could easily be drafted.

When did you first meet Nasrin?

I don't exactly remember but it was though Guthrie – one friend said there was an Iranian lady there. Zahara was young. We were not close, we didn't do a lot, we were both very busy, and my boys were in travel soccer. I got to know her when we reconnected when our kids were at university, and we became much closer. Our kids were at Iliad High School together too. One son went to CU to study Biology, and is in Medical School, the younger is in New York City the director of sports marketing. They are 31 and 32.

We usually spent time walking to Stewart Park, and drinking coffee like we are doing. She was always very, very positive and optimistic and very hard-working. Stricter in a sense, because you do everything for survival. You come here and you work, you had to find opportunity. We are not scared of anything anymore. You provide opportunity for our kids and hope that they never have to go through what we went through. They (the kids) don't understand what we're talking about. We are proud of our kids.

Did you spend any Iranian Holidays together?

We had some, but for the most part we spent them with my family and my husband. What I like about Nasrin is her honesty and I felt very comfortable. With her honesty, she was trustworthy. My husband and I have a lot of friends. You have other friends that are social. With trust, you can talk about everything and have confidence that it would stay there, and that was the major thing: if I was upset with someone – and she'd never bring it back to my face. And we could speak the same language, it was easier to communicate. We had a similar situation from our kids that brought use close to one another. Bringing up kids was our primary job, not the profession, the kids were number one, I feel that strongly. We say *Bachan* –"my love", something that is part of me, more than that. She was concerned that Zahara would have a good life. She got married, has a good husband and family, and she has such a good heart. She's educated, and a good daughter.

I went to the burial ground yesterday to plant some flowers. I feel comfortable to visit there. It is a comfortable spot.

Did you ever experience discrimination?

Never, it never affected them or any of us. Iliad is a very diverse place, best thing for Nasrin and I, even in California and Madison, never had a problem. But it's a different culture. In California there is one or one and a half million Iranians in Los Angeles. Even with people on staff from the small rural areas, I never had any issue, and I don't think Nasrin did. Maybe we were lucky. With Susan, Noni, Carolyn, you, I feel comfortable, I told Siman, Zahara is with *the good moms*. Zahara is more comfortable with Nasrin's friends – she always mentioned her friends – so proud – than family because she has not been exposed to the family as much as the mom's friends, and they were really there for her, all the time.

When Nasrin was going through chemo, and after, her mind was making her anxious, she was stressed and anxious and we started meditation – we went for 3 or 4 months – and the other friend, Sorayya. Then I stopped going because I had to come from work, but when we walked, we talked about it, and the meditation really encouraged her to change her mind. She was a single mom. You get sick. What's going to happen to Zahara? She had courage, she took care of all of her family, and it was a lot of pressure, but she enjoyed it. And the meditation gave her time to herself.

Why did she come to the US?

She got married and her husband got the job at CU, they came to San Diego first. But we never discussed this in detail because it was not a happy time. He had an affair. Her husband was young. Nasrin didn't know anything about radiology, but right after she got her divorce, someone guided her to the field and she decided to go back to school. I met her husband once, at Zahara's high school graduation. The husband was a family member. Siman knows him too.

Did she have any English when she came here?

She came here and had no English, maybe some basic English at high school, moving to a new country it's a whole new world and the culture is different, culture shock, and you have to start over. Nasrin was very strong, I always admired her, and during her sickness. She was firm but direct – persistent about her diet and everything. She had a very strong personality, but because of this bad experience in her marriage it was hard for her to trust another partner, and she didn't want to bring someone to her home with Zahara. Deep down she could not trust [another man]. I wish she had had someone.

How did you learn about the US?

In Iran, in other countries compared to the US, you learn about the educational system you learn a lot about politics. Here high school students don't know where the countries are on the map and they think the only language is English. There is more curiosity, especially in Europe: it's part of growing up. My father studied Flemish. I went to an American School [in Iran]. The US and Iran had a very good relationship with the Shah until 1978, then the military came to Iran, and financial transactions. The US relationships changed. Money was coming here, but without the product (probably military product) they could not even function. It was making everyone angry. There was a gap between the lower middle class. Then the students took over the Embassy, and their ideology was close to that of Russia's. The US was very scared that Iran – we had so many resources and were always at the center, and there was China, Russia – whoever would grab the resources. The US was afraid Russia would take over. The US government played a role for the Shah to leave – he lost his strength. Carter wouldn't let the Shah use arms against the students. There were so many students. It became like a power vacuum. The government could not put the students in jail, and the students were close to Russia, so many kids close to that ideology. There was a riot in Egypt, and the Shah went there, and Khomeini got power. We never had that in our history: a priest comes to power and takes over the government. No one thought it would last. After that I say anything is possible. We were saying: *Look at this type of people!* Laughing. *Why those guys are like this?*

Nasrin went back to Iran to visit.

Because she had her mother there. She was a normal citizen. Even if I go back, this is information. Iran has information on all of us. They would know. But I am in *Grants and Contracts*. They can take you even if they know your parents have done something. Nasrin lost her father when she was 12. He was in business. The younger brother had a store – appliances, like *Bed Bath and Beyond*, the older one was in real estate, and her sister's husband, jewelry. Her parents too, real estate. They never worked for the government so they are safe. They – H. and family – come here every few months. They don't want to emigrate, but they want opportunities for their kids. Their kids are so smart. Like Zahara.

My family is in California and they don't want to leave. I can't imagine going back. Nasrin comes from a different city – it is green, near the water, from the north. I am from the capital. When I left the population was 3 million, it is now 13 million. Our house was torn down and now there is a high rise. It is like Iliad turning into New York City. Nasrin and I came here when we were students, 22 or 23, if you ask me now to move to another country, it is impossible, my family is in Iliad. I like Iliad. I know my doctor. Convenience. I cannot imagine going back to Iran. Iran is a different country.

Nasrin's family – the father was in business, and she was not encouraged to go into the business. Siman got married. Nasrin was the only sibling that went to college. Nasrin was self-motivated, and always wanted to try something new. But when the family come, their primary motive is money. They are never content. Nasrin was content with what she had. She wasn't interested in money: she loved her house and Iliad. Her brother and sister are interested in money. The family is very good at business. Nasrin left very early on in life. She was the eldest and the favorite of her father and she even looked like him. When her father passed away, she felt the responsibility of her family, all her life, even with the colon cancer, even helping them get the green card. As the eldest, she wanted to protect them. She did everything for them.

But her father's death left her feeling anxious for the future. She would advise me: put some money aside you never know what's going to happen. Don't put off doing what you want to do. She was always worried for her future. It makes me more comfortable with my ageing. Still after the meditation – it was much better.

The love that she had for Zahara, that's how she did it, made it here: it was an amazing relationship. I was in the room when Nasrin died. Zahara kissed her and cried. I have never had that experience. Hospice care came that day and said it would be soon. She died at 7:30. She suffered, and was resistant to death, finally she said, *Zahara, could you bring me some morphine?* I never saw any child love her mother this much. Mine would never. Zahara was in a very bad situation, but she was protected by Adam. She got the best person in her life. I never thought I would be able to do it. I closed Nasrin's eyes. H.'s wife was there to cover her. Zahara said to get rid of all the medicine. We did, then we called hospice care.

I woke up the next morning and I thought *How am I going to handle this?* But I had to be with Zahara. We saw burial places and the service place and we did everything in one day. It was an amazing experience for me, I had never been with someone at the passing moment. Nasrin had pain, she was bending over in pain, but that was what she wanted, and I admire Zahara. One thing I would have done, knowing that she's passing, I would have given her medicine. She never accepted her death. There was only a phrase, *I'm dying*, she said in Persian, in her unconscious. Another friend came in and said, *Are you her sister?* And Nasrin said, *My sister, my friend, my everything.*

Zahara amazed me, what Nasrin has raised and given to society: smart, humble, loving. I admire her for raising such a good kid. She left her job, she drove back to Iliad every other week. Toward the end, it was very hard caring for Oliver and her mother. Noni helped with all of the arrangements – she did all of the research. All the energy of the forces helped us.

Nasrin had not prepared enough. She worked so hard. Nothing was easy for her. It was hard work at Guthrie, getting in at 6. And what I loved the most about Nasrin – her generosity. As we get older people get attached to our money. Not Nasrin.

I have a picture of her, all made up. That's how I want to remember her. I think about what she told me: *Do whatever you like. Don't postpone it. If you really like something, just do it. Just be yourself and do whatever you want.* She became very present in the moment. She enjoyed walking and her time with her grandson. Don't worry so much about the future.

16. Carolyn, phone, 7-29-2019.

Tell me a little about yourself.

I was born in Iran, which was an important link that Nasrin and I had. My family moved here when I was eight. I grew up in the Midwest and lived in Chicago and I got into yoga and studied ballet for a long time, and ended up in a lot of different places and yoga organizations. I met my husband, Bruce, there, and ultimately, we disengaged from the organization and we moved to Iliad with another couple that we're still friends with. We lived in Iliad for 18 years. That's how we got to know Nasrin. Then we moved to Virginia and I became an officiant, in fact about three years ago I ended up officiating Adam's and Zahara's wedding. Then we moved to Hawaii four years ago.

Do you remember the first time you met Nasrin?

Absolutely. We lived on Comfort Road in Danby and the person next door, who was at the corner of Gunderman and Comfort, somehow we met them, and they said, "There's this other Iranian woman who is renting from us, living in the basement apartment." I wasn't sure I wanted to meet another Iranian. Nasrin felt the same, we thought it might be show-offy, and neither of us were in that mode. But then I met Nasrin walking, strolling Zahara down the roadside, who at the time was about one-and-a-half, and we *had* to talk. We knew who each other was, so we introduced ourselves and we became fast friends. For more than 30 years, till she passed away. I just adored her. She didn't have a bad bone in her body.

Do you know who owned the house?

The people who owned the house--it was 35 years ago--no one is around that long anymore. She moved there with her husband when she was pregnant, and he was so wrapped up in his stuff. And shall we say he was not whatsoever supportive of her? Nasrin was pretty much on her own, and she did a marvelous job. She was amazing. He eventually left, and left her penniless. He wanted to become a citizen and marry someone, an American. Ironically Nasrin went through all the right channels and became a citizen before he did, if he ever did. He was good to Zahara when he would come, he did care about her, that's a good thing.

Nasrin was amazing. There was a time when she was working for 75 cents-an-hour and she didn't take any public assistance. Such a smart, determined and ethical person. Honest. One of her favorite things to me when we were talking – she used to call me Caroline – which was my original name, my name before my passport was changed. She used to say, "Can I be honest with you?"

Yes, I know.

Are you kidding? I'd rather that than anything-- of course you can be honest with me! It was such a cute expression. She was just a sincere soul. We had some nice long talks before she wasn't able, before the family came, she was going downhill, and she was tired, but long talks, and she was just wondering why this kind of thing would happen to her. I told her sometimes we are incarnate here, and our job is to take others' pain, that I feel that you have been this sponge of absorbing family pain, and that you are sort of the chosen one. In that respect, because Nasrin was in every way or form I can imagine, a beautiful soul. She was exemplary. We go through life getting mad at people and she's the one person I would never ever get mad at. She was a spotless person. I still love her dearly. Yes I love her.

Do you know why she left Iran?

It was to get married to Bahman. He was a brilliant man, a scientist. The family knew each other, they were from the same town, Amol, in northern Iran, by the Caspian Sea. I don't know if it was partially arranged, partially accepted. He was here going to university. They were married remotely?

Yes, on the phone.

Then she came to California. He got a post doc at CU, and they moved to Iliad.

Do you know if she knew anything about the US before coming over?

The popular image of the US would be that it was this wonderful place, this land of plenty. She didn't come from a poor family, they were well-to-do. You were going to go and your situation was going to get better. It happened to my family too. But there was this magical image as to what this place was like: there couldn't be anything wrong here, that it would be a wonderful place, a wonderful experience. I don't know how it was for her in California, but she did meet people there, and there were certainly a lot of Iranians. Iranians are very well-educated, and she met a lot of people who became life-long friends from California, some who were from similar places in Iran.

Do you know when she came to the States?

I don't remember what year they came to the States, or when they came to Iliad, but Zahara was born in 1987. I don't remember how long she was in California.

Do you know if she had any English?

I also don't know, but if she did it might not be much. She picked it up quickly. She was young, but not young enough because she retained an accent that was ingrained in her twenties.

Would she have learned English in school in Iran?

No. My family spoke English, my Dad spoke seven or eight languages, my Mom, five. We were in a different situation: my family was Christian, and they from northwest Iran, a little further west than Nasrin's area. There were the Christian missions from the US: Presbyterians who came and brought education, hospitals and medicine. We spoke Assyrian because we were Assyrian, and we spoke Farsi because of Iran, and we spoke Azerbaijani because we lived in that territory. And we spoke another language. My father spoke French because it was the international language, Russian because Russia was right there. And there another language. Anyway it has to do with where you live and the culture and it was not unusual for people to speak three or four or five different languages. Nasrin spoke the language of Mazandaran because she was from that province, and it was a little different; she used to call it my *city language* that was different from Farsi because she spoke two of them plus English. She spoke three languages. It was just the circumstances, unlike the US where you come here and everybody speaks the same thing and that's all you know. I won't go into that.

My family spoke English because that was part of their educational experience, and I'm not sure about Nasrin's experience or as to what extent in Azerbaijani, but being that they were Muslim, so they wouldn't have been exposed to the other Christian languages which were American. I don't know if they spoke English, my Dad worked with the British so that made his English even stronger.

What were some of the things you did with Nasrin?

Just hanging out. It didn't matter, we could talk forever when she was on her own with Zahara. Later we moved away, we had both moved from Comfort Road. My son was almost exactly two years younger than Zahara, so we'd hang out. We were like family and sometimes Bruce, my husband, would babysit the kids and Nas and I might go out. It didn't matter. One time we did go to the Renaissance Fair with my son and Zahara, the four of us. Sometimes we'd go to the zoo in Syracuse or the Carousel Mall and ride on the carousel. Just to hang out. She met my dad, who'd visit, and they had a funny thing going. One time my dad said: Every province you make fun of: *We have some jokes about Mazandaran*, and Nas: *Well we the have some about Azerbaijanis.* And she quickly let him have it really fast, and we all cracked up. It was really sweet. We had the commonality, our experiences were different in Iran, religious experiences were different, but this commonality was like a family, there were certain things we understood, a link, that was really special. There was no one else I ever knew like that, like my own family.

She was definitely a soul sister.

How long did she live on Comfort Road?

He left, and she stayed a little, then she moved to Nancy's on West Hill where the neighbors were the K.'s and they were good to her, and Nancy was pretty good, but she was also feisty. Sometimes it was hard. Then Nasrin bought a house on West Hill, and some years later moved to East Hill.

How did she get the babysitting jobs?

Between us and Nancy and Noni, she got a lot of emotional support, as far as financial, she pulled herself up from the bootstraps. I don't know if she got financial support from her family; she did not receive her part of the inheritance because she was a woman, and she wasn't there (in Iran). I don't think her family had any idea of how she was living. They assumed anyone here was wealthy and that she was doing really well. She'd always take a lot of gifts when she'd go there. I don't know how she got those jobs or decided to become an X-ray technician but she took Zahara with her until Zahara got in school. She studied and did well. She was a smart woman, flying under the radar. If there was anything Nasrin had, it was determination. She suffered a lot, but she didn't give up, things did open up for her, but it wasn't as if she didn't work her ass off. She was quite inspiring in that way and look at the way she brought up Zahara – she was awesome super-loving but firm. She just loved Zahara.

And she wasn't afraid of death, she told me, we talked about that, but she didn't want to leave Zahara and Oliver. That was the hardest part for her, if you've ever had the flu you think, *I'm ready to die,* forget it. It was love that went beyond personal misery and cancer. She loved them so much.

Maybe she told you the story of the grandson coming to her in a dream?

No.

She was ill and she had the cancer, before Zahara got married.

Diagnosed in February, 3 years ago.

Nasrin must have been doing chemo and she was working on Zahara's wedding dress and Zahara said, *Mom, you don't have to do this*, but that was giving her incentive to live. And she had this dream about had a grandson pinching her butt, and she said, *What are you doing?* and he said, *Isn't that what grandsons are supposed to do? Pinch their grandma's butts?* That was a sweet dream, and she did have a grandson after the wedding, if you believe in those kinds of things -- a soul to come in and bring Grandma joy.

How has Nasrin's death affected how you live?

I can say that one thing it makes me more aware of my mortality, and I had better savor my moments because you never know. How it's affected me otherwise? It makes me very sad, it hasn't been that long, because we were separated for so long, we didn't see each other but we spoke on the phone, and when I think about her being gone it makes me very sad. I pray for her soul, still, wherever she is, and well-being, held in the love of God. I miss her dearly, one of my old friends and a strong heart connection, and the thought of her being gone just feels ridiculous. I said to my husband: *It's inconceivable, I can't believe she's gone.* I've kept her texts, I don't have a voice message. It's heartbreaking but it does make me want to be more grateful for my life. Thank you for asking the question.

Has her death made you think more about dying and how you want to die?

It's going to happen, I don't know when or how but in terms of being at peace with myself and the world, those are the conditions I would like to meet. I would like that kind of business to be taken care of before going. I don't want to take that unresolved junk with me, wherever it is I am going. (Laugh) That's really important.

How do you mourn? Personally.

I get sad. I'm not one who cries much. I care deeply and I get melancholic when I think about it, and she's sort of, aside from my parents, my important loss at this point. One forgets that they're ageing, I'm ageing, it could happen to me, to anybody I love. The fear, I try not to go with that because I know that whatever our assignment is, by coming here, the final assignment is to leave here. But that doesn't make it any less sad when someone you loved has fulfilled their assignment, so it hits me sometimes. It doesn't seem real. I try to not think of her as being erased from existence. She still exists for me and I know her soul is there. How do I mourn? Not with complete annihilation: I mourn because I can't talk to her, I can't pick up the phone and talk to her and that makes me said and I miss her.

I know Zahara is going to hear this: Your Mom loved you deeply, and Oliver and Adam very deeply, and Bruce and I too, and Lukas. We're your family, and we hope we can be of some support.

18. Virginia, phone, 2-28-2020.

Tell me about yourself.

I was born in Argentina and came to the United States in January 1985 to do my Master's in Anthropology. I had a Fulbright Scholarship at SUNY Binghamton. Before that, I spent all my life in Bella Vista, a town 30 kms from Buenos Aires City. I always lived with my parents until I came to the United States. I was 26. I met my husband right away. He was also studying in Binghamton. At the end of that year, I went back to Argentina first and he followed. We got married in January 1986. He's from India – Nasrin also knew him. Then we continued studying in SUNY. In December of that same year our daughter, Anita, was born in Argentina. My husband tried to find a job in Argentina – he liked it very much, but he couldn't. Eventually, he got one in Groton, near Iliad. We lived in Iliad for six-and-a-half years until we got our green card which then seemed to take forever, but nothing compared to what it is now. My husband couldn't stand the cold anymore and he read about Austin, Texas, and thought it was going to be a good place to raise our kids, with cheaper housing, etc., which it isn't now, but was back then.

When did you come to Iliad?

I came to Iliad in December 1990, after spending two years in Argentina. I had a J visa with the Fulbright, so I had to go back to Argentina after completing my studies to fulfill what I had signed. When I signed the contract, I was not married and had no clue about the implications of a J visa. It ended being that I had to stay in Argentina even though the Argentine government told me *You are free, we don't need you, you can return to the United States* (in other words, I was exempted), but the US Secretary of State said *You have to abide by what you signed,* so I stayed put in Argentina two years, living with my parents and my daughter. Just at the end of those two years, my husband, who was still in Binghamton, got a job in Groton and rented an apartment in West Village Place in December 1990. We were in Iliad until July 1996.

My daughter went to C. Heights Elementary, Kindergarten to 3rd grade, and in Austin, she did 4th grade, also in a public school. After that, we looked for a school with high standards and found a small Catholic one. We didn't have enough money to pay the full tuition, but they gave us a scholarship. Anita met April there and we became friends with her parents.

What are you doing right now?

I stopped working in 2015. When I came to Austin I had to work, and I couldn't find any thing in Anthropology, so I applied to publishing companies, but that did not work out. Teaching, I decided, would be perfect – same schedule as my children. I taught in elementary school as a bilingual teacher for 10 years. Then I joined Pearson, a global publishing company, and worked there for more than eight years. In 2015, they lost the contract with the state of Texas – after 30 years – and laid off many people, including me. But it turned out alright, even though I was not of retirement age, I was planning to stop working the following year. Since then, I do projects like family history, writing about my family, and things that I never did before: exercise, yoga, zumba, and helping my daughter when she got married.

Do you remember the first time you met Nasrin?

It was at a birthday party, or at a meeting at the elementary school. Anita was invited to Zahara's party when they were living near West Village, on West Hill.

Both of your daughters were in the same grade.

Yes. We went to Cass Park with our daughters or she would come over for dinner or we would go to her place. She was busy and I was busy, so it wasn't as though we had a lot of time for ourselves. We did not have time to go out, for example, to have a cup of coffee. We did everything as a family so that our daughters could play together. Maybe it was the first year we met when she asked if I could look after Zahara during the summer, because Zahara was out of school and Nasrin was working. *Yes, of course*, I said. I was not working, I preferred to be home, and babysitting was one thing I could do. After those two years of not being with my husband, I wanted to make the best of our place: decorate the apartment and be fully dedicated to the family. It was the three of us together after so long, imagine. I think we agreed with Nasrin on two or three dollars – something that she could afford and helped me at the same time. It was mutually helpful.

Zahara spent the whole day at my home and recently, when I was in Boston, she said: *You kept us busy with activities for math and reading*. They were little, first grade or end of kindergarten, I just did not want them to watch TV because I am not a TV person. I wanted them to play and create things, and at the same time have academic activities. Nasrin would come and pick her up and we'd always talk, always very, very close: we'd open our hearts and say everything. No secrets.

One day Nasrin came home with a pile of shirts that needed to have the collars fixed. She asked me if I would like to do this job with her and I said *Sure* (I do not remember who gave it to her.) We got about $50 each for the whole pile. We were so happy! It was more than a week worth of groceries.

Did Nasrin talk much about Iran?

No, she would say that she was not happy at all with the political situation after the Shah of Persia was thrown out. She really thought it was crazy what they were doing with women, and the whole situation in general. She was very proud, she always said *Persia,* not Iran. I noticed that she wasn't talking Persian to Zahara. She was proud, but at the same time, was not expressing those feelings openly like I do with my country of birth. I am always talking to my children about Argentina, and we only speak Spanish among us – even my daughter and son speak Spanish to each other. I think she had mixed feelings about Iran.

Did she talk much about her marriage to her husband?

Oh yes. I met her when Zahara was four-years-old, at that time she was already divorced. She was studying to take the exam for technician certification. The first time, she failed, but she persisted. It was hectic because she had to study, work, take care of Zahara, had little money. Sometimes my husband would help her with the car – it wouldn't start in the morning, it was a very old car; winter in Iliad, imagine. Not fun. She had friends who helped her, but she struggled.

I want to tell you before I forget, that I used to cut her hair. I was giving my husband a haircut, and my daughter, and she said: *Oh please, can you do mine?* I said: *I'm not a professional at all, I just use the scissors. Just cut it*, she told me. It went from long hair – when I met her – to short.

Can you tell me how Nasrin has impacted your life?

She was very smart, very bright, and kind. I admired her because she was clear; she knew right away what was right, what was wrong. I do too, but you know she was more decisive. That's what I learned. And to say things, to take care of yourself, to give yourself importance. For me, I think of her as being very gentle, and I saw how important that is, to smile and be sweet, and at the same time be true.

She was genuine.

Yes, genuine and gentle. Always be very respectful, for example when we started talking about the weddings, and my daughter was with her boyfriend, she would always advise me to be cautious. When you see those traits in another person, even if you have them too, you pay even more attention to them, and those traits are strength.

She was very sharp. Straight away, she knew immediately what to say, even if she didn't know it for herself, she would give you good advice. She struggled; sometimes she would say she did not know what to do, but mostly she was very clear.

Decisive.

Yes, something opposite to myself, indecisive.

Her death and its process: how did that affect you? You were in Texas.

We were in touch with messages. We would talk on the phone until she couldn't talk anymore. I told her not to worry about answering. Even if she could not respond, I would just send a picture of a flower, an icon, or a few words. We were in touch. I admired her because in spite of getting ill just before Zahara's wedding, she kept going. She was so happy when Zahara got her Ph.D., I could see how thrilled she was to share that moment. Wedding plans were right after that, and then the sad news. She was extremely nervous and I understood her perfectly. We had shared our fear about illness on different occasions in the past; we were alike in that respect. That gave both of us peace of mind; especially now, I think it helped her to know that she was not the only one.

And how it affected me – her death? It was sad that she couldn't enjoy her grandson. She died so young, such a beautiful woman. When you say Nasrin, I see her eyes, the expression in her eyes. Zahara also has big eyes, but they are not the same. Nasrin was beautiful. Those eyes she had were special, wide-open, alert, and sweet and warm at the same time. Incredible. Nasrin and I always talked about getting together. She said, *Come to Iliad, have fun*, but she was working and I was working so it was very hard to find a time to do that. Then came her illness ... and I went with my whole family to Zahara's wedding. The following year Nasrin came with Zahara and Adam to Anita's wedding; that was the last time I saw her. Then Zahara came again to Austin to visit my daughter, and I asked Nasrin: *Why don't you all come?* But she was going to Iran. After that, she became very ill and I didn't want to go and see her because I thought, *If I go now, she's going to think that her end was near*. It was very hard for me because at the same time I wanted to be with her.

Has Nasrin's death made you think about your own death?

Yes. Actually, I went to visit Zahara last October and I stayed with her in Boston in the same room where Nasrin had stayed. I was thinking about her being in the room, and I looked through the window and thought, *Oh my God*, wondering what she was thinking and of course I thought, *Yes, it can happen to anybody.*

Has Nasrin's death affected your sense of spirituality?

I have always been very spiritual, and it hasn't changed. Her death did not decrease nor increase it. I know Nasrin was leaning more toward spirituality; not that she was not spiritual before, but she talked more about that in her last years. We didn't talk about religion when we were younger. I wish we had.

Would you mind describing how you grieve?

That's another very good question. Actually, I think about that ... *what is grieving*? How would you explain it?

For me, grieving is a way of making my life seem right again without Nasrin, but still having Nasrin with me and her memories. In my own way, I read and write, and that helps me make some sense of death.

Well now, I think I know. For me, the best thing was to go and visit Zahara, and talk with her. That was something I wanted to do. Zahara always told me *Come whenever you want.* And for Christmas, after Nasrin passed away. Zahara said how much we meant to her, that we were like family. She has a lot of memories of us. When she said all that, I felt she needed company. Going to Boston and spending time with her was something that brought me comfort.

I didn't go when Nasrin was near the end as I have just told you, so I felt that going and staying with Zahara and just listening to her, being with her was the best thing to do. She talked and told me a lot of things. Spending that time with her and her family gave me comfort. I felt that I was doing something good for Zahara and for Nasrin.

Here people talk a lot about what they do for grieving. I don't recollect that as being part of a conversation when I grew up, even though there were several deaths in my family. When a person dies, you are sad, and you keep going. You pray or you don't pray, you mourn in different ways, but we don't talk about grieving. My husband has the same recollection from India. Seeing it from an anthropological perspective, I think it's a cultural thing.

Do you want to add anything else about Nasrin or your relationship with her?

Again, her eyes. Her eyes said everything about herself: gentle, kind, bright, sharp. I would say all what I told you already: they add to her understanding of human nature. Yes.

19. Susan W. 7-19-19, in person.

Tell me about yourself.

I'm 69 years-old and I've lived in Iliad for 43 years and I love it here. Nature is my spirituality and the abundant natural beauty of this area feeds my soul. I had the amazing good fortune to meet Nasrin about 25 years ago and she blessed my life with her friendship. I work as a care giver at Comfort Keepers. As a nurse, I worked at the hospital and also at Guthrie where Nasrin worked. She helped me get my job there. I am semi-retired and do limited home care.

What's your earliest memory of Nasrin?

My earliest memory of Nasrin was at the Ellis Hollow Fair. I remember her saying she was thinking about applying to dental school in Buffalo. We may have met each other at Lukas B's birthday party. Lukas was in my daughter Laura's class at Caroline Elementary School. His Mom, Carolyn, was a friend of Nasrin's.

What drew you to Nasrin?

Her friendliness and her delicious Persian cooking. She was interesting and interested in being friends. We were both single Moms and our daughters became friends.

What did you do together?

Dinner the first time, I think. I was over at her place a lot. First on Hook Place and then on Terrace View. I live on Snyder Hill, about a mile from Terrace View. She was always inviting me over. When our daughters were young, they'd put on skits they'd choreograph and dance for us and we'd video them. When it was just Nasrin and I, we'd walk our dogs (Abby and Hershey), stop in at a little sandwich shop called the Coal Yard Cafe near Nasrin's, go get ice cream at Sweet Melissa's, confide in each other about what was on our minds, watch *Dancing With the Stars* or *The Bachelor*, among other things. Occasionally, we'd go on little trips. Once we took our daughters, who were probably around 10 and 12, camping near Boston. They had the strange idea that we'd take them clubbing in the city. They spent at least two hours in the camp bathroom getting dolled up for a night on the town. Nasrin and I got a kick out of that. They ended up sitting in the car for a couple hours and didn't seem to mind that being their big night out! Whenever I went to Nasrin's, she'd bring out food, even though I'd make her promise that she wouldn't feed me or wait on me. As she was setting out food, she'd say, *No I'm not doing anything*, and I'd say, *No, you're waiting on me.* You don't know how to relax. [Here Susan shows me a photo on her phone of Nasrin, Zahara and Adam, Spring 2018 or 2019 She's a very nice-looking woman.

Beautiful.

She's always been beautiful.

Do you know why she left Iran?

She got married over the phone to Bahman, who was in California. She was coming to join him. I am in awe of her courage to come here alone and leave everyone and everything familiar! I think she probably intended to have a different life from what Iran allowed for women.

Was this an arranged marriage?

I don't believe so.

How did she meet him? Did she know him from school?

He was around her family in Iran. The marriage wasn't arranged. She never used that term with me.

Do you know if she had any English before coming over?

No she didn't, as far as I know. She didn't know how to make a bed, much less speak English. They had staff and staff did all the cooking and cleaning until her Dad died when she was 14. She didn't know the language, the culture, the money. She didn't know anything about what she was coming to.

How did she learn English?

When Nasrin and Bahman separated and she had to make a life for herself and Zahara, she started babysitting and cleaning houses. She took care of two children. She started learning English by watching Sesame Street with them. In a short time she became proficient enough in English to apply for an X-ray Technician program at T. Community Hospital (CMC's name at the time) and she got accepted on a scholarship, I believe. To become so adept at English, that she could understand medical terminology in a short amount of time, I think Nasrin had superior intelligence. She was academically intelligent and became socially and culturally intelligent quickly. She had the determination and courage to persevere and make a good life for Zahara and herself. Your first language indelibly imprints on you. She did mix up her English pronouns at times; she for he and he for she. Occasionally it was confusing to follow. Her choice of words would make us laugh sometimes – with Nasrin.

How has she affected your life?

Instantly her generosity comes to mind. Generosity requires energy. It was a miracle to me, how she could work for six days a week for 20 some years and still be there anytime, day or night, for her friends. For example, I remember having a car problem at the bottom of Buffalo St. one cold, snowy night. I called her and it seemed like seconds after I had hung up, there she was coming to my rescue. There's a wonderful country song entitled, *Find Out Who Your Friends Are* that describes Nasrin perfectly. I'd mention the slightest disappointment (much less a major setback in my life) and she was there, dropping something off at my front door – food or a little gift – to support me or just to remind she cared. I remember saying *I'm having trouble finding basic black flats*. And the next day, there was a bag at my front door, not only with black flats in it but also another pair of cute blue and white stripped summer shoes as a sweet extra. That type of thoughtfulness and generosity just touched my heart. It happened so many times. I would say the slightest thing to her that indicated some need and, if it was within her ability, she would do what she could to make it happen, even though my intent was just conversation. I started editing my concerns because I saw her inability not take it on as her responsibility. I imagine I am just one of many friends that she took care of like that.

Your friendship with Nasrin has made you a better person?

Absolutely, or at least made me aware of my need to try to emulate her. Nasrin modeled the attributes of kindness, concern, generosity and selflessness. Her life is my inspiration to develop those qualities in myself.

Did you talk about Iran?

She talked about her summer place on the Caspian Sea. I wish I had taken notes from every conversation we had about it because it would have been the most beautiful, rich book. I guess I thought she would be around forever to share those stories. I certainly wanted her to. The summer place sounded magical. When she was there on her last trip to Iran, she sent me a picture of her and her Mom sitting at a picnic table. It was a lovely, touching picture of them together.

I met her Mom during the summer of 9/11. Her Mom was reluctant to come even though Nasrin had wanted her to come for years, and she chose the summer of 9/11. She dressed in black and wore a scarf. She didn't speak a word of English and I obviously didn't speak a word of Farsi, but her Mom and I connected instantly. After 9/11, she wanted to go home immediately. She was going to take a bus to JFK Airport all by herself. The times were tense and Jim F., my fiancé at the time, in his generous way, insisted on driving her to JFK. At the airport, she gave me a little piece of paper. I wish I still had it. "May God keep you safe", it said. I knew then and there where Nasrin got her loving ways! I was so touched and carried it in my wallet for months until my purse was stolen. It brings tears to my eyes to think of that moment even now. There are good people in every country, and I am proud we did that, a little contribution to peace and love in the world.

Another time, I was coming down Snyder Hill and I noticed Hashem in his car, pulled over by a policeman. I stopped and started crossing the street. Hashem spoke hardly any English. The policeman met me in the middle of the road and I told him I was a friend of Hashem's and his English was limited, and asked if I could help. He said everything was fine. Then I saw the policeman leave and I followed Hashem back to Nasrin's. He had been stopped because his passenger (an Iranian man) was not wearing a seat belt. They were ticketed. I accompanied them to the C.U. police department and it was resolved. The passenger had released his seat belt to reach something on the floor and forgot to put it on again. Hashem never forgot that I stopped because every time I saw him after that, he gave me a huge bag of "Iran bread". Lucky me! It's delicious!

Nasrin took Zahara back to Iran.

She wanted her to know her family, especially her Grandmother. Nasrin wanted to take care of her Mom and bring her here. Family was important.

After this experience, have you thought about death more?

I think about death differently and a lot. In retrospect, I wish Nasrin had taken the morphine sooner. At the same time, being the person she was, who honored her body and ate healthfully and avoided medications, it made sense that she waited two weeks before dying to take the morphine and give herself relief from the pain. She brought the same courage to dying that she brought to living. The way she died was a manifestation of the hardships and battles that she confronted in her life. I don't think any day was easy; she was frequently up against challenges. She had the fortitude to keep going and keep her head up; to put one foot in front of the other and carry on. That was one of the things she would say to me often about difficulties and unfairness: *That's ok.* She wouldn't swear or get mad.

How do you mourn someone you had known for so many years and so well?

I feel the pain of her loss as a huge hole in my heart. I miss her every day. For the first nine days, I went to the cemetery every day. I felt like I needed to help her adjust to her new state. I actually verbally introduced her to her new "neighbors". It seemed right, knowing how focused on others Nasrin was. But I have to let her go. I don't in any way want to interfere with the peace she's found. She's released from her earthly cares. She's escaped the clutches of cancer and I hope she's safe in her Dad's arms now. I don't go daily anymore. Maybe every two days. Some nights I'll go two nights in a row. It's comforting to have a place to feel close to her. Sometimes I bring flowers. Initially, I thought I have to go because this is the closest I can get to her physically. One night I brought a shovel to plant some flowers and had this crazy thought of digging her up. The visual of me in jail brought me back to my senses, so I quickly planted the flowers before locking the shovel back in the car. I know H. was caring for her grave also. Zhila and Houseene too. We all do a little bit and I go there and know someone else came and that is comforting. Every time you go there, it's a little different. Someone else is bringing flowers too. Someone else planted six little petunias. Three groups of petunias, little gifts of beauty for Nasrin, become balm for the pain because someone else showed up and remembered her too.

20. Zahara, phone, 4-1-2020.

You must be pretty busy these days.

With a newborn and Oliver it's definitely hectic but it's also a beautiful time. Remi's asleep on me, and Oliver is chatting in the stroller.

How are the boys doing?

They're doing pretty well. Oliver is really sweet with his brother. Remi is a little more relaxed than Oliver was or maybe I'm more relaxed. Oliver has been having somewhat of a tough time with the transition, the first few weeks because he had me all to himself, but he's getting better.

How do you think you have changed as a person since your Mom's passing?

It all blends together. Since her diagnosis, by watching her go through this illness, I've become a more compassionate person. With others going through tough times I used to feel awkward reaching out to them, and now I want to be there for people in any way I can. I realize how much it means when you're going through a tough time to be there. I feel like so many of her friends like you have been amazing and that meant so much.

My priorities in life are completely different. I used to work a really stressful job and I wanted to work my way up the ladder and make a lot of money, but none of that matters any more. I want to be happy and healthy and be a really good mom to my children. That's the best. After I quit my job, I haven't had a single regret.

There's some good that came out of this, but since her passing I've also felt more lonely, she made me feel as if I had a whole world of people who loved me; after she passed, I realized it was all her, and that's been tough to navigate – being in a world where you don't have that level of support and love and care and understanding. It's tough to get used to. So there's good and bad.

You mentioned earlier that before your mom's passing, you were a very happy person. How would you assess your level of happiness now?

Before it was probably a 10, now it's 7, 6.5 or 7. I think I'm still average, I don't feel complete joy, I have moments of it, but I don't feel that anymore. It's a beautiful way to live if you can see the beauty in every moment. Losing that is tough but I have hope that I will get back there. After she passed there was six months where I was really depressed. Getting back to more normal, even if it's not joyful and loving every moment of life is still a big improvement, so I have hope that it will come back.

What is your outlook on life at present?

I have always believed that life is beautiful if you let things fall into place, beautiful things will come your way, and if you have a challenge, it's an opportunity to learn, or a way to direct you on a better path. I try to bring that to the present moment, but I definitely struggle with it more than I did before. I have more anxiety than I did. Sometimes it's hard to let go and trust that things will work out. Before I thought everything would work out and then one of my biggest nightmares just came true: everything might not work out beautifully. That's a scary realization.

Are you doing anything to center yourself? Other than being with your immediate family?

I try to go for walks everyday which really helps, being in nature. In the past mediation has really helped, I feel like I got into it, now I feel like I'm just going through the motions and it's hot helpful. I hope that it becomes helpful again. And it's tough to find time to do much, if I can get a walk in, hopefully as the kids get older, I'll have more time for myself.

Do you have any other thoughts on your mom's passing that you would like to talk about?

Some things that just generally come to mind, beautiful; things, like reflecting on her life how much love and compassion she brought to the world. It's been inspirational for me and her friends, to continue on, that's such a beautiful thing that she left for us. But at the same time, reflecting on it, I think it is so important to take care of yourself and not put other people and their well-being above your own. That's an important lesson. And to value yourself, and that's something I wish she could have done more of. Sometimes I wonder if the outcome would have been different if she had done for herself a little bit more.

21. Noni, 11-24-19, phone.

Tell me about yourself.

I grew up in Iliad. I lived in various other places, California, New York. I work in on-line education.

How did you meet Nasrin?

I was living in California and I came back to Iliad and Nasrin was renting a room from Nancy, which was next door to my parents. Zahara was in a highchair then. It was probably Nancy who said, *Oh, you should meet my housemate because she has a daughter similar in age to yours.* At some point I moved back to Iliad. I remember Zahara sitting in a high chair and being fed by her Mom. I first lived at my parents' house and so I saw Nasrin often.

You became friends because you had a daughter around the same age?

You could say that, and she was in the neighborhood and she didn't have, she had a pretty unusual situation with her husband. The entrée was because we both had children.

Did she tell you much about her husband?

I met him back in the day. She told me a little why she left him – he had taken up with another woman.

Do you know what Nasrin was doing to support herself?

At some point she started going to school, but she was watching someone's kids and she would take Zahara with her, and she somehow got into the X-ray Tech opportunity. Sometimes I think about Nasrin – this whole period when she was living in California, which I don't know about. As for the Iliad living, she was in a house in Danby with her husband, then she left him, moved to Nancy's house, then to a house on Hector, then another house on Cliff Park downstairs (Sue's) for quite awhile. She lived at my parent's house between houses then I heard she bought a house on Hook Place. Zahara was probably around eight.

Did Nasrin ever tell you the INS story?

No.

Did she talk much about Iran? Why she left?

She must have wanted to leave. (We talk for a minute about her marriage).

She mentioned to me feeling jilted by someone she had loved. Then years later, a rebound?

Yes. Rebound. She tried to get back together with that guy again. She wanted to start something new with him. Didn't she study for her medical degree? To my memory, she was studying to be a doctor.

I know she attended Empire State (in NY).

This was in Iran. I think she was studying medicine, and because of her own natural anxiety plus her father's death, she could not finish her studies.

Her brother, Hashem, mentioned something about her teaching health to students in Iran.

I don't know, but certainly she was always working in health-related fields.

She went back to Iran when Zahara was five. Do you know if she was hesitant to go back? If she was scared?

I'm sure she was scared to go back, that something would happen at the border, that she would have to stay. Her mom visited right? She wanted a natural connection / communication with her mom. It was sad about her mom, her mom had this classic vintage house and people tried to convince her to modernize it, destroy its character. She and her brother and sister disagreed with Nasrin. I don't understand the internal family dynamics, and by being far away she didn't have as much pull, and the house was a source of sadness and frustration, understandably so.

How has her death affected you? Has it made you think more about your own death?

For sure. She's my first close friend who died of a sickness rather than by an accident. We actually had time to watch her illness progress and time to reflect on life's choices and regrets of things we did not communicate to each other, and then the sudden realization that we have to take advantage of it. I'm not at peace with the choices she made, but she really felt that it was not her job, that it was God's job. When her life was cut short, remembering her comment about Hershey, her dog, that it was *God's job* helped me understand a little bit about what went on. Zahara and Adam supported Nasrin's wishes. Once when we were driving, Nasrin said, *I have a pain, I feel something here.* It was frustrating that she had not wanted to share that information with her doctor. It was a mystery to me, her choices.

Has her death changed how you feel about death?

Preparing for my own death certainly. There was a moment when I was researching Muslim burial, and I gave Zahara some options, traditional and non-traditional. The Western route. You'd would want to discuss this with your kids, I think.

It was not easy to have conversations about death with Nasrin because there was this thought that the conversations could propel her downward. (Note: her spiritual advisors did have conversations with Nasrin).

I was hesitant to talk for the same reason.

Are you spiritual?

No. But I feel very sad that she had to leave us so early. It's amazing all of these emotions, there's an underlying – frustration? Frustration maybe about the way medicine works.

What else do you want to say about Nasrin?

I'm finishing knitting the blanket that she made for Oliver. In typical Nasrin style, it is huge. Have you ever seen it?

No.

I'll send you a photo.

Yes, I'd like that. So what drew you to Nasrin?

My mom was also an immigrant, and my husband. I have a lot of experience with people coming to this country and having to readjust their life, and there was a kinship there, even though we were parents. Zahara was a year ahead of Maia at school, but they weren't in the same social groups. I tried to interest Nasrin to send Zahara to the Waldorf school. I really liked the school. I'm an alternative gal at heart, but she wasn't interested, she was much more going toward an academic education. There were a lot of things we didn't share opinions on. We would still get together on holidays and birthdays. I have lots of videos of Zahara's birthdays and things like that. Nasrin didn't have a family here and we became her family. In general, my family tends to adopt people, so Nasrin just became part of the family. It was not even a question. I treated her more like a sister than a friend. Even while knitting, I'm swearing at her: *What the hell were you thinking? This is enormous!*

She was a finisher. It gave me funny frustrations—watching her rake leaves, for instance. She liked to finish things. I have lots of stories. I'm trying to do that for her, with this blanket. But I'm a little out of my depth, and I'm sending it back to Zahara to have someone block it.

22. Debbie, over the phone, 7-14-19.

Tell me about yourself.

I was a nurse in Iliad, now in Michigan I am a nurse practitioner, after returning to school. I came to Iliad with Bill, my husband at the time, he was going to CU. This was in 1984. My first job was with T. Community Hospital and I worked in the Labor and Delivery Unit. My first son was born in 1987, Jay. He was babysat at first by a young girl who answered a flyer, then by some lady in a trailer. I didn't like the lady's house, and the girl was not ready to take care of an infant full time. I got my son into a daycare, but it wasn't the greatest situation. Twenty-two months later, I was pregnant again and had Adam in December 1988. And we looked at Coddington Daycare on East Hill, but we couldn't afford to have two there, so I put an ad in the paper and Nasrin answered. That's how we met Nasrin. My husband at the time was a grad student, and started doing programming and moved from getting the Ph.D. in English to Computer Linguistics. By then I was working at Planned Parenthood, so were both working a dayshift, and we could no longer share childcare responsibilities.

Nasrin was our god-send.

You remember the story I told at the Memorial service? The first time she came to interview at my house, it was without Zahara. And she said: *I have something very serious to share with you, and you might not want to hire me.* And I thought: is she a criminal? *There are two things: I have been through a divorce, and I have a daughter and I have to bring her with me.* Just like that. And I was okay with that.

It was meant to be: she (Nasrin) was born on January 23, born on my stepmom's birthday. She started working that next week. That was a big thing: she needed money. I had six weeks maternity leave and I started looking for someone around the 4th week. She stayed with us until we left Iliad in '91, because of the cost of living in Iliad, and we had family in Michigan. We needed to get back home and I got a job in Detroit.

I wasn't sure if they were okay with animals. We had two dogs and two cats, but Nasrin loved dogs, and she was fine with cats, but the cats probably aggravated Zahara's allergies. And she was scared of them, but once she wasn't, she liked the cats. Zahara was really timid as a kid, and she was scared of men. She did not feel comfortable around men, although her playmates for those years were Jay and Adam. It took her a long time to warm up to my husband. She never spoke to men. When we were getting ready to leave for Michigan, Zahara spoke her first word to Bill-- in those three years -- and it was something simple, but he was flabbergasted. It was monumental to him. For some reason we were walking down State Street, meeting at Planned Parenthood, and they were crossing the street and he said: *Take my hand and look both ways okay?* and she said, *Yes, I am fine.* And he was like: *Oh my God-- she spoke to me!* Actually, she probably didn't catch herself in time. It took her a long time to warm up to anything. She never, never spoke to men, but she spoke to the boys all the time.

God bless for Nasrin for taking care of those three little kids. A newborn, a one-year-old, and a two-year-old. Cute to see them all together, and she did it with grace, and ease and had fun with it. She had an old clunker car, and was nervous about taking the three kids. When she able to afford a better car, she asked to take the three kids out, and I said okay! All those kids in car seats. They would go on outings and field trips. We also had strollers and the kids walked.

I lived on Westhaven, 131, beside Cindy M. [Author's note: I live at 135). There were rolling hills in back and an apple tree. I cannot believe how much land you have lost. At the time, Nasrin lived in the basement of Nancy's apartment, it was a dinky moldy apartment with mildew. It *was* moist, but she could be independent. Zahara had a thick green mucous coming from her nose and never breathed out of her nose for the first two and a half to three years! It was terrible! Just terrible! She was quite congested. We laugh about it now. But Nancy was a little odd. Then Nancy moved to Ecovillage.

After we left, we'd come back almost every year and rent a cottage along the lake and see Nasrin. I had two nursing friends, Kate and Sue, and Sue T. had a son, Luke. Sometimes he'd come to the house. There's a story about Nasrin putting one of the plastic kiddie pools in the front yard. It was flat there. There was this pudgy, pale red-haired boy, Luke. A lot of baby fat. They all wanted to swim, so she put the four kids in the pool. Luke didn't have a suit but he wanted to swim and Nas didn't want his clothes to get wet, so he just went in. He had one of these disappearing penises. Nasrin and I laughed our butts off over that. She had a great sense of humor.

All I needed her to do was watch the kids, but she also had the laundry done, the dinner cooked. She'd take the kids up to Flaccos farm and watch the horses and pick up treasures around the fence. All sorts of things. I'd come home exhausted and she'd have dinner on the stove, and I'd say: *Oh Honey!* and she'd say: *Not a problem.* We'd never had Iranian food before.

God, she was a godsend.

We'd talk on the phone because seeing each other only once-a-year was not enough. She would call me *Dear,* and I noticed Zahara is doing that now – taking on her mom's thing of calling me Dear.

We met in Iliad in March of 2013 or 2014, with Mark, at a bar on The Commons because I wanted her to meet Mark. She gave her approval – so to speak – and that was cool and it meant a lot to me. Zahara was in Ann Arbor, University of Michigan, doing lab work, and Bill and I took her to lunch – that was a blast – and let her know that if she had any problems, that we were there. It was neat how we kept up over the years and being one-third of a country away.

We talked on the phone about her diagnosis. Nasrin had a medical background from Iran, more technical and hands-on, but that did not count and basically she had to start over. She lost everything – all her training and degree – but it wasn't hard for her because she knew what she was doing. I'm not sure where she got her training – maybe in Pennsylvania or TC3. She worked at T. County Hospital first. She had two part-time jobs. Her supervisor wasn't so cool, and so she only worked at T. County Hospital on weekends. She was such a damn hard worker. She did not complain.

Then she started doing the facial treatment at Hook Place, on her balcony or where the sunroom was [Terrace View]. I never heard of anyone using string to trim eyebrows. She said: *Come into my spa,* and I did.

At Hook Place, her Mom visited for a whole summer and that was tough on her. She spoke not a lick of English. Zahara didn't speak Farsi. I give Nasrin credit for that, her mom and all. The mother covered herself up and that was different. Her mother would not leave the house.

So Bill stopped coming to Iliad, he didn't want to go to the cottages, he was a butthead, so the others came alone to the house for dinner. Nasrin had slow-cooked all day long, trying not to tell them what they ate. They ate venison! And it wasn't tough or gamey. It was funny. She was so gracious. She'd say: *You have to have a cup of tea.* And I said to her: *You need to relax.* That's what she was like. One time I left she gave me rose water and said: *It's going to relax you.* At the funeral I saw one of the cookies made with rose water. Oh my god, I thought: this is so Zahara and Nasrin.

Why did she leave Iran?

She had an arranged marriage with butthead. She was on a visa that had to do with his visa and if she was divorced, she could have been deported, and she did not want to be deported. She did not want to take Zahara back to that under any circumstances. It was a weird time in Iran. She applied for citizenship. During early in the divorce and she had to prove that butthead still lived with her. Immigration came in and looked for clothes in the closets and toothbrushes, but this was at the transition of the divorce, and I think he refused to move out. It was not a good time. [Note: Zahara was 16 months old when Nasrin found B.'s car at someone else's house in downtown.]

Why did she stay?

America had a lot to offer, and she wanted to protect her daughter, and did not want to have to take Zahara back to Iran.

She had a lawyer in New York City who was doing the citizenship work. He was not ethical. Nothing was moving along. He kept asking for more money and my stepdad, Uncle Don, was a lawyer, and they loved Nasrin, and he thought this doesn't seem right, this should be happening faster, so he made some phone calls or complaints to the bar. The next thing you know things started moving faster. And that finally became resolved and she finally became a citizen. It was a long process. It pisses me off, Americans who take advantage of foreigners. This is a woman and she's going to fight this. Nasrin persevered. Good for her. She did not back down. She knew people who knew people. She was a very, very smart woman, and knew how to navigate [life]. It didn't matter if we didn't see each other for a year, it was almost as if we knew each other in a different life. We always said: *God gave us each other.*

She was Iranian, she could have been Muslim, but she was Christian. She helped me decorate for Christmas. I didn't know much about Iran. I knew she came from money enough to pay off the bad people, so her brothers weren't killed. They had an estate, but her family was taxed heavily. The government tried to get as much money as they could. In the earlier days, I did not understand her English, so I did not ask questions. I didn't want to get her in trouble, and I didn't ask questions that might be painful. She would say that her daughter is never going to have to cover up like that.

How did she learn English?

Practice. My son, Jay, was very verbal. Jay talked a lot--he could tell you stories about the love lives of others! And they watched Sesame Street.

Nasrin could not go into the family business. It was not acceptable. It was very traditional and Nasrin didn't like that. Her marriage was arranged, he was from the family. They were weird times in Iran. Sometimes a woman could be educated, sometimes not, it depended on the regime. Same thing with young, and going out in public and being covered up and the bullshit about the arranged marriage. She was a woman and you could only do so much. She didn't have a choice, she had to follow her husband. Nasrin was an independent woman. She did so much for herself and Zahara, but she struggled, it was hard, and she did it. I am so proud of her. Man. Yep.

She gave me such support, especially through my divorce. We talked about the problems with our marriages.

Our medical background connected us: it was a nice togetherness. I told her about pap smears and when this thing with the colonoscopy appeared, she got it. She understood. She wasn't clueless.

23. Sue, her home, 8-16-19.

Tell me about yourself.

I am from Penfield, New York, which is a suburb of Rochester. I have lived in Iliad since 1976 with my first husband who had a job at the hospital. I worked at CU, secretarial work in Ag Economics, before I had kids. We lived initially on the hospital grounds in townhouses nearby, then for a year we lived on Hyatts Road. We bought a house in '78 and we bought this house in '85.

How did you meet Nasrin?

After we moved into this house, we turned the downstairs into an apartment. We had one fella here who worked for the general (hospital) for a while, less than a year, then he went back to New York City. Nasrin and her husband answered our ad in February of 1986 for the apartment. They had been living at the Ramada, now the Holiday Inn. I was hesitant about a couple living here that did not speak much English, but it turned out to be the best thing that happened because she helped me so much. I've had MS since '76 , symptoms diagnosed in '79. We got very close. Nasrin was up here all the time, she used to bathe Laura because she was one-year-old, and my son, who was four, and she helped a lot.

About 10 months later, next January, she informed me he'd gotten a job in Canada and she was giving me two weeks notice. My first husband, Bill C., put an ad in the paper and we found another couple to rent, and then Nasrin contacts me and says the job is not working. For quite a while he actually never did work; he had a job at CU but he was trying to finish up his Ph.D., which meant money was hard (to come by), but they both came from wealthy families and she was sent money from home, that was how they paid the rent. We felt bad so Bill and I decided, why not let them live upstairs? We thought it would be a couple of weeks, that they would eventually move to Canada. We had four bedrooms upstairs and they lived in the furthest room. There was a washer and dryer. After they moved upstairs, Nasrin was not feeling well: turns out she was pregnant with Zahara. Her husband was not around, turned out he was at CU where he previously worked, playing pool and things like that. Nasrin was cooking downstairs and we liked her food, and she cooked for us too. After seven weeks, they were still here, and it was a mutual decision at that time. They moved out into the motel on Rt 13, on the way to Elmira. They'd just redone it and there were kitchens, but it ended up being more money than they were told, so he found an apartment on Comfort Road in the basement. Zahara was born when they lived there. But it was way out, she was used to taking a bus into downtown, so she was stuck at this place and couldn't go anywhere. There wasn't any bus, and she didn't drive, and living in that part of town wasn't good for her. The basement apartment had high basement windows and one time she found a snake down there. Things like that.

Again he was leaving her quite a bit, and he wasn't working, and he had no green card, and never did anything about the green card even after they were married. They lived in LA for a while and there were many Iranian people that she got to know, and I think that's why her English was sparse. She used to watch Sesame Street to learn.

I remember visiting her in this apartment, and he said to her, shortly after she had Zahara: *I found this girl, or woman – a* student he used to tutor – who said: *She'll marry me so I can get a green card*. I'm sure most of what he told her wasn't true. They divorced, he married this girl and they moved to California, I don't know for how long, and I don't think that helped him get his green card.

So after she left that apartment she wanted to go somewhere closer to town.

He left her at Comfort Road?

Yes. So he leaves her and marries this girl. Now Nasrin needed some kind of work, and I knew of another apartment – we had long ago rented our apartment to other people. Do you know Nancy B.? She lived on Richard Place and raised five kids, she had a situation downstairs, two bedrooms and a bathroom, and I don't know if anyone else ever lived there, but she met Nasrin and really liked her, so the two of them moved in. Nasrin ended up – well she was not happy about this – cooking every meal and doing dishes. She also paid some rent and she was watching Debbie's kids up on Westhaven which wasn't that far for her (about one mile up a steep hill).

One night when she was over there, and I used to take my kids up there, especially my daughter, Laurie, and they would play and they got very close, the police came to the door and arrested Nasrin. She was here illegally. I don't know if Nancy lent her money to get out of jail. How did the police find out? I think because they got divorced and they knew she was here. He probably had a visa – that's how he was over here for school, because she was married to him, and she was on the visa, or something like that.

After that and after Debbie moved to Michigan, Nasrin needed another job so she was watching twins on the bottom of Hector Street in this little house that they rented. The woman worked at Tops in the meat department cutting meat. I went to visit. They rented the upstairs of the house for a year or so, then after that she bought her house on Hook Place, probably with help from her family.

I forgot a whole part. I just remembered Nasrin decided to go to the hospital's Radiology School – somebody might have talked to her. Zahara might know. That would have been in the early 90's, she had gotten some degree before that in Iran. A two-year degree? She wanted to do something with her life. Before that she went and hired a very expensive attorney to get her green card. For her to go through all of this, for a woman by herself and from where she was, and actually accomplish it, it was unbelievable. She did have some things that weren't good that happened to her at the school. I don't think she was working while going to school, and for two years we opened our downstairs and family room, and Bill offered two years for no rent. That worked out. The only thing was we could smell all her food, and of course Laura would be downstairs sampling. She pretty much stayed down there. We were more apt to do down there – Laura and I – to visit. Every day Zahara was going to the West Hill school to PreK and she'd get off the bus and I'd stand at the sliding glass door so the driver knew I was here, and I'd have her after school so that helped out Nasrin.

Earlier she had helped me. Then when they were living downstairs, I know she was friends with Noni because she'd come over and visit, that's how I met Noni. Nancy B. lived next to Noni's parents. It would be nice if this could all come together.

It was disappointing when we went to her graduation at the hospital and Nasrin had been the top student. Two other people were given these nice scholarships and they said they were the top students. Did they acknowledge her as the top student? No. She was upset about that.

Now that I think about it, Nasrin also had some health problems. She had surgery, she was gone suddenly and we went to visit her. Appendix? I don't remember. But I do want to add something: he (Bahman) and I had some terrible arguments. He was 10 years older than Nasrin and he basically spotted her and said, *I want to marry her*. He eventually divorced the wife from California, then he moved to Tennessee. At some point he got bladder cancer and Zahara and Nasrin went down there and stayed with him. He may have had a lady friend with him then.

Maybe it was an appendicitis that she had. She didn't take any child support and was not offered any. Why don't you fight him for child support? I said. *Oh no*, she said, *because he'll want to split custody and I don't want that to happen*. So she didn't fight it. With the colleges and all, he never came to graduation. He stopped calling. Zahara got to the point where she would call him once in a while: *I'm getting married*, and things like that and: *I'm coming across the country with Adam*. I don't know what was going on with him. Zahara called him up when they were getting close to where he lived and she said: *I'd like you to meet the man I am marrying. Can we come over?* He said no. He's never met him, he would not even let her come. So what was he hiding? There was something going on there that he didn't want her to see. No one knows what he's doing.

Nasrin always ate so healthy and she walked. Nasrin is the last person I thought would get cancer.

For a long time when I first knew her after they split up, we talked on the phone nightly. After I married Bob, and we got busy, we would still catch up, she felt like my kids were her niece and nephew. She was like that. As they got older, it was harder for them to visit. Laura lives in Middletown, about two and a half hours away. Dean lives in Iliad. They were both at the funeral.

Do you know how she learned how to drive?

I taught Nasrin how to drive, but I don't remember about when that was, it must have been after they split up. I think she had driven some at home but it might have been a stick shift. We didn't have to work at it too long. I remember the day she passed, but I don't remember what day that was.

Did anyone help her buy her first car?

I have no idea. I don't know anything about the first car I don't even know what it was! She always would find cars that didn't cost a lot. She got one that was sitting here in Pete's parking lot, and she went in and asked about that. I don't even know if it had a *For Sale* sign on it. She did end up buying that car. They might not have lasted her long, but she found cars.

She just was such a nice person. She would do anything for me. One time she met my parents and in-laws and I remember my father saying that: *That guy ought to treat her right – she's an attractive lady and she could find another,* but she had trouble finding other guys. I know she wanted to be with somebody again, husband or whatever, but I think she wanted to wait until Zahara was older. It just didn't work out, and I feel bad that it ended that way. The other thing is: she loved her daughter to death, but that grandson: I'll tell you that one picture Zahara took of her holding Oliver when he was more of a baby, that looks so much like Nasrin. I know she wants more kids, but I don't know how she feels now. She was in Boston and she's building a house here, I don't know if that started yet.

How has Nasrin's death affected you?

Well it's very hard not to be able to pick up the phone and talk to her and see how things are going with Zahara and Oliver. We used to talk about everything. I wanted to add – you might know this – she was never treated right at any of her jobs. She was a supervisor at Guthrie. They treated her so poorly and I really think it has to do with her being foreigner. She used to say she came from Persia, she never said: *I am from Iran.* That I know. When she came over things were really bad and anyway, that wasn't fair to her. Guthrie treated her very badly. Too bad she couldn't have sued them. She was out on sick leave with cancer, and they tell her she has no job to come back to. I remember that.

Has Nasrin's death made you think about your own death?

No, I guess I don't feel about that now that I have had this little stroke. I am 66 and my parents both died at 69.

 One time, and again, it was my first husband, was taken up to Strong (hospital) for a heart problem. They took him by ambulance. I had to get packed quickly and I am one of these people who puts the sheets on my beds, and I didn't want to leave without the clean sheets, and here she came right over, and helped me pack and she actually made the bed with me. I could always count on her. You know how she was not here for my birthday in July – it's the same day as her Mother's. One year her mother came over. It was nice: she had dinner for both of us even though her Mother couldn't speak English, of course Nasrin could translate.

I didn't see her at the end. What was it like? Was she able to talk?

The last time I saw her she was in bed and asked for water. I did not talk to her. There were a lot of other people there.

About a month before, she asked me to take her on some errands and at that point she was 82 pounds. I could not believe how small she was. She walked into the bank so slow and when we were in the car, she took her shoes off and she put her feet up on the dashboard. They were hurting her so bad and I thought, I wonder if it's in her bones?

Do you know if she ever wanted to go back to Iran?

No. She knew things were not good. I think what she really wanted to do was bring all her family over here, and look what she accomplished. I was wondering, after she passed, if they'll keep coming here every 6 months? Some got green cards. She worked a long time to get them to come over. Her mother didn't want to come back; she didn't like it here. Her sister doesn't speak much English, but her nephew and niece do.

Another question, Sue: How do you mourn?

I did cry at the funeral. Seeing different people that I hadn't seen for a while. I was so glad her sister was with her that week before she died. Because of my MS – I've had it over 40 years – I've been doing pretty good with it, all these years trying not to get stressed out. So I haven't been good at mourning, meaning I haven't been sitting and sobbing. I hate to cry.

Acknowledgments

I would like to thank everyone who gave their time to be interviewed and trusted me with their words, their personal thoughts and feelings: Sarah, Anna, April, Hannah, Adam, Ben, Julia and Shiv, Hashem, Carolyn, Debbie, Noni, Alice, Virginia, Sorayya, Marie, Zhila, Yasamin, Carole, Sue and Susan. And thank you from the bottom of my heart, Zahara, for the permission to write this book and for your help with contacting Nasrin's family and friends.

Several people read my earlier drafts and gave me solid constructive feedback, some feedback that set the book on a different and better course: Jonathan Frankel, Tammy (Airbnb guest), Beth Dickinson, Sorayya Khan, Jeanne Lawless, Leo Tohill, Diana Ozolins and Jeanne Coyne Song. Zhila, during our interview, provided the inspiration for the book's title. Mike Drury, Lauren Ostergren and Jeanne Coyne Song proofread my manuscript. Thanks to Lisa Kilgore for her help with formatting the manuscript and cover.

Thank you to David Farber and George Bonanno for permission to quote from their books. Similarly, thank you to those from the *On Being* podcast who also granted permission: Joe Henry, Jonathan Rowson and Gordon Hempton. My boss, David Fernandez, graciously allowed me to work part-time and permitted me to take Fridays off for the past few years. Thanks to Terry Fleig, high school buddy, for writing encouragement over the years. Finally, I'd like to thank Mike, Ben, Laura and my European traveling companion, Anna, for all of their love and support.

I am indebted to all of you. Now go out and live your life, and make the world a better place.

Made in the USA
Middletown, DE
07 December 2021